A Journey

*An account of the life of Peter Hồ Văn Mây,
Vietnamese refugee and Catholic priest in
Canada*

By Gilbert Taggart

Victoria, British Columbia

Note for Librarians: A cataloguing record for this book is available from Library and Archives
Canada at www.collectionscanada.ca/amicus/index-e.html
ISBN 1-4251-0790-7

Printed in Victoria, BC, Canada. Printed on paper with minimum 30% recycled fibre.
Trafford's print shop runs on "green energy" from solar, wind and other environmentally-friendly power sources.

10 9 8 7 6 5 4 3

This book is dedicated to
Father Hồ's new grandniece

Claire Hồ Thanh Trúc

Born in Victoria, British Columbia
June 21, 2006

May she share the faith and the
values of her family and her great-uncle
and honour their Vietnamese heritage.

Table of Contents

Author's Note...3

I. Places...5

II. People...11

III. Preparations...20

IV. The Narrowing Path...43

V. Escape...55

VI. Survival...81

VII. Prospects...102

VIII. Way Stations...110

IX. Adaptation...132

X. Milestones...146

XI. The Road Beyond...154

XII. Going Home...166

XIII. The Guide...180

Author's Note

Every human life is a journey, even those spent in one small corner of the world. In these days of increased mobility of individuals and populations, it is not unusual either to find people whose journeys have carried them afar and who have lived in many different areas other than their place of birth. I think we do not always realize what is involved on a personal level in these successive adaptations, especially in the case of someone like Father Hồ who has been constantly in pursuit of a specific goal from childhood on. For this reason I think that Father Hồ's story deserves to be told, which is what I have attempted to do in this summary account of his life up to the present.

My wife and I would also like to express here our appreciation to Father Hồ for all the occasions, both joyful and sorrowful, in which his presence has touched our own lives.

In this text I have attempted to respect the original orthography of names and quotations in Vietnamese. Special markings of the letters can change entirely the meanings of words and I would not want any Vietnamese reader who comes across this book to interpret them in some unexpected way, which might sometimes have unfortunate consequences!

Vietnamese biblical quotations contained in the text are from the authorized edition of the *Kinh Thánh Tân Ước* published in Sài Gòn in 1994. English quotations, I must confess, are from the King James Version of the Bible first published in 1611.

Gilbert Taggart
Victoria, British Columbia
June 7, 2006

I. Places

Father Peter Hồ, pastor of St. Patrick's Church in Victoria, Canada, was born with the birth name of Hồ Văn Mây, January 23, 1944, in Tân Hòa village, district of Thanh Bình, parish of Bến Dinh, province of Đồng Tháp, Việt Nam (Vietnam).

Let us begin by situating these two geographical points.

Victoria is the capital of the Canadian province of British Columbia, though not its largest city, which is Vancouver. Victoria is located at the southern extremity of a large island off the western coast of mainland British Columbia called, somewhat inappropriately, Vancouver Island, since the metropolis of Vancouver is situated on the mainland. Victoria is a rather quiet city of some 300,000, enjoying a mild, almost Mediterranean climate. Tourism is an important local activity. Victoria is also the retirement destination of many Canadians, and the average age of inhabitants considerably exceeds the national average. The city is strongly marked by British traditions, but is also home to an active French speaking minority. As in most Canadian cities, there are also various immigrant groups, including a Vietnamese community.

Việt Nam is to be found on the other side of the Pacific Ocean, at a more southerly latitude, occupying the coastal region of the Indochinese peninsula. Việt Nam is only part of the former French Indochina, which also included the protectorates of Cambodia and Laos to the west. Each of these countries became fully independent after the departure of the French in 1954. During the colonial era, the borders between them were of somewhat lesser importance, as they all fell under French administration and there was frequent trade and communication among them. For example, the former Catholic diocese of Phnom Penh, the capital of Cambodia, also included parts of southern Việt Nam. Beyond these areas to the west, and separated from them by either mountains or dense tropical rain forest, lies the ancient kingdom of Siam, known as Thailand in modern times. As for Việt Nam itself, the shape of the country has been compared to that of a dragon or a phoenix or, more graphically, to a bamboo carrying pole with baskets of rice at both ends. The northern "basket" corresponds to the former French protectorate of Tonkin, of which the principal city is Hà Nội, the present capital of Việt Nam. The slender "pole" in the middle is the region formerly referred to as Annam, the principal city being Huế. Finally, the southern "basket", which is truly a food basket for the country, comprises the former colony of Cochin China, including the city of Sài Gòn and the rich alluvial plain of the Mekong Delta.

With its source in the Tibetan highlands and a total length of some four thousand five hundred kilometers, the Mekong is indeed a mighty river. As the Mekong flows into the sea, it splits into a number of waterways, continually depositing huge quantities of silt to form and extend the Mekong Delta, a process which results in the delta further protruding into the South China Sea at the rate of about 80 meters a year. This delta, one of the largest in the world, is for the most part intensively cultivated, principally for rice, but also for sugar cane and various fruits and vegetables. Each year, extensive flooding occurs from the beginning of August to the end of October. Although cultivation must cease during this period, the flooding brings fresh sediments which ensure the richness and productivity of the soil. Temperatures are warmest from February to May, often reaching a daily average of around 30°C. They then begin to decline as the summer monsoon season begins. The delta has a very high population density: almost 40% of Việt Nam's population of eighty million live in the delta area.

But let's sharpen our focus and move closer to the map of the Mekong Delta. One of the two main branches of the Mekong is called the *Tiền Giang* or Upper River. Coming from Cambodia, it crosses the northern part of the delta before splitting into some seven different estuaries at Vĩnh Long. The province of Đồng Tháp lies astride the Upper River, stretching from the Cambodian border to a point not far from the river's division.

This is indeed a beautiful area where people and nature live in perfect harmony. Intensive cultivation of neat little agricultural plots furnishes subsistence to many families. Nearby there are forests of mangrove and bamboo giving haven to numerous species of birds, including storks, cranes and herons. Transportation between the villages and towns that dot the countryside is often by boat because of the periodic flooding, when the mighty Mekong practically covers the land.

The parish of Bến Dinh, one of five located on an island in the Mekong some thirty kilometers long and only three wide, has today been divided into two: The Holy Family (Thánh Gia Thất) and Saint Andrew's (Thánh Anrê). The land had originally been purchased by a French priest and subsequently given to his Christian converts. Today the island's total population is around 30,000, farmers and traders for the most part. Their homes are stretched out along both sides of a road running the length of the island, with the principal church located in the center. A sense of community is very strong here: the people are hospitable, charitable, friendly and polite. They support each other in any way possible, especially for events such as weddings and funerals. The life of the Church is very important to them: Mass is attended faithfully, and each parish has its own school, where the much loved Sisters of Divine Providence dispense instruction to every child.

The Vietnamese people in general, however, have not had an easy time. The fugacity of human life is a well accepted reality. Centuries of political conflict have only added to the burden of eking an existence from the land, however bountiful it may be. The last century, in particular, was an extremely difficult one, as a great war between worldwide political forces was fought on Vietnamese territory and the Vietnamese were the principal victims, whichever side they may have found themselves on. It is not surprising that their religious faith has been a crucial element in their ability to carry on and perpetuate the human condition in this sorely tried corner of the world. Indeed their continued faith in God, as reflected in their adherence to one or another of the great religions, has been a shining example to other peoples of the earth. These religions constitute a complex socio-cultural mosaic which is a tribute to Vietnamese tolerance and generosity.

Hinduism was the dominant religion of the Cham people who founded a flourishing civilization in the South which lasted until the 15th century before being engulfed by migrations from North and Central Việt Nam. The remnants of the Chams converted mostly to the Muslim faith, but retained many of Hindu practices. Confucianism, introduced during the ten centuries of Chinese domination before the 10th century, has since been a dominant force in determining the Vietnamese social and philosophical outlook. Buddhism is perhaps the most widely practiced religion in Việt Nam today, along with related beliefs such as Taoism, Hòa Hảo and Cao Đài (Caodaism), an ecumenical movement combining facets of other major religions. The latter two, unfortunately, have in the past also had political and even military aspirations which have not always been compatible with the beliefs they profess.

Christianity, primarily Catholicism, was introduced in the 16th century by French, Spanish and Portuguese missionaries. The Church was often persecuted in the succeeding years but continued to grow and manifest its vitality, particularly during the French colonial period. After the end of the recent war, the Catholic Church was viewed with great suspicion by the new government, which imposed severe restrictions on the ordination of priests and the practice of religious education. These restrictions have been eased somewhat recently, and the Vietnamese faithful have set about the imposing task of restoring churches and institutions which had fallen into disrepair during the period of repression. In this, they have been aided by financial contributions from Vietnamese expatriates and other outside sources. Today the Catholic Church is regaining its place as a force for moral good and the source of personal salvation for some 10% of the Vietnamese population, the highest percentage of any Asian country except the Philippines.

II. People

Now we return to our account of the journey to the priesthood of Hồ Văn Mây, baptized under the Christian name of Phê-rô (Peter) Hồ (Vietnamese places the family name first and the given name last, while the middle name indicates male or female, or has some other symbolic significance). The young Mây never knew his grandparents. His mother, Lê Thị Phạn, came from a Christian family, but his father, Hồ Văn Ngự, came from a Buddhist tradition, his own father having however been given up for adoption to a French Catholic priest at an early age. Lê Thị Phạn died in 1970 at the age of 55, but Hồ Văn Ngự lived to the age of 86 and passed away in 2001. Their family consisted of six boys and four girls. Four children, Hồ Văn Ren, Hồ Văn Hóa, Hồ Văn Hoài and Hồ Thị Đậm all died at an early age. One of the boys, Hồ Văn Đỏ, attained the same age as his mother, 55 years, before his death in 2004. The remaining brother, Hồ Văn Tòa and three girls, Hồ Thị Án, Hồ Thị Trắng and Hồ Thị Đẹp continue to live on divisions of the small family property in Tân Hòa village, where they cultivate rice and vegetables and raise chickens, ducks, pigs and cattle to supplement their meager income.

The family has always been deeply religious and practiced their religion scrupulously. Father Hồ remembers that every day began and ended with a family prayer. For his father, who tended to the many tasks of a farmer, this often meant rising as early as 4:30 in the morning. On Sundays, the whole family walked to the church, a distance of three and a half kilometers, and of course the same distance coming home after Mass!

One Sunday, at dinner after their weekly journey, Mây's mother Phạn told her son how proud she would be if someday he might become a priest and say Mass and give Holy Communion. It was a theme to which she gently returned almost every Sunday. Little Mây had only a very vague idea of what this meant, but slowly the desire to accomplish his mother's dream took root in his young heart. He loved his parents dearly and was a daily witness to their spirit of sacrifice and self-abnegation. These sentiments were moreover shared by the entire community, and when Phạn passed away in 1970 and Ngự in 2001, thousands of mourners joined the funeral processions. This respect was certainly well deserved, for what greater gift can parents give to their children than the desire and ambition to live a life of service to fellow men and women.

What do you have to do to become a priest? Mây wondered. He guessed you had to go to a school and study a lot, but for the moment he didn't think too much about that aspect. He spent his time looking after the cattle in the pastures and helping his parents work the farm during the harvest season. When not otherwise occupied, he engaged in games with companions of his age, playing hide and seek, making mud pies and, not infrequently, conducting solemn ceremonies in which he and the others pretended they were priests and altar boys.

However, it was not always pleasant and peaceful on the farm. As this was an area only recently claimed from the wilderness for cultivation, it still had many of the characteristics of a "frontier" country. Security and protection against bandit attacks were sadly lacking. These attacks often occurred at night. When there was fear of such an attack, mothers would quickly gather up all the important possessions and flee with the children to the protective cover of nearby bushes, where they would hide until the danger had passed. The bandits, whose identity was well known in the village, would often demand protection money in return for refraining from an attack. If this was refused, they would return night after night in the hope of finding the family treasury. On one occasion, bandits forced their way into Mây's home before anyone could escape. All the adults were blindfolded and tied with their hands behind their backs to poles and chairs, whereas the children were made to lie flat on a table and stare at the ceiling. "Unless you tell us where the money is," one of the bandits snarled at a terrified Mây, raising his machete, "I'll cut you into three pieces!" Only a shout from one of the other men announcing that money had been found in the basement prevented him from carrying out this terrible threat.

Such threats were to be taken seriously. Although fathers were well versed in the martial art of Kung Fu and other defensive tactics, they were often no match for a band of knife-wielding bandits and some lost their lives defending their hard-earned savings. The story is told in the village of one such attack in which a particularly notorious bandit murdered both members of a couple while plundering their home. An older son managed to escape, but the bandit went unpunished, although he made no secret of his crime. Later the son joined the French army and rose to the rank of captain. He returned to the village with a company of soldiers and sought out the bandit, who was seized and dragged to a spot in front of the church. A crowd had gathered, fully expecting that the bandit would be executed. However, the son unexpectedly pardoned the man, stating that his Catholic faith did not permit him to take the life of another, whatever his previous crimes, and that the soul of every human being, even that of a murderer, is worth saving. At first, the crowd reacted angrily to this act of clemency, but the example of Christian charity and spirit of forgiveness was not lost on them and there were subsequently many conversions to the Catholic faith. The number of parishioners grew steadily from about 1500 in the 1950's to more than 10,000 today.

Among the other dangers faced by the villagers was the ever-present risk of a grave illness striking some member of the family, particularly the children. In addition to malaria, transmitted by the swarms of mosquitoes that breed in the swamps, diseases such as cholera, tetanus, meningitis, typhoid and dengue fever are all endemic in the region. Even today, visitors are advised to take appropriate precautions, for they lack the resistance to these diseases which the native population has acquired through constant exposure. As a child, Mây himself did not escape the danger. He fell dangerously ill from an unidentified disease to the point where he lost consciousness and all signs of life seemed to have disappeared. An elder in the community who was well-versed in traditional medicine was called in to see if there was any hope of saving the child. The elder, after verifying that the patient was indeed still alive, went into the fields to collect certain herbs which he then administered to the comatose child. Fortunately, with this repeated treatment and the patient care of his mother, Mây eventually recovered consciousness and gradually returned to health. Today he credits the elder with having saved his life.

Having succeeded in getting most of their children through this exceedingly dangerous period of early childhood, the parents turned their thoughts to how they might begin their education. For Mây, it was decided that he should spend a year at a boarding school operated by the French Soeurs de la Divine Providence, located on an island about thirty kilometers down the river.

So one morning in 1952, Mây's father took his son on the beginning of his journey to the priesthood: a boat ride down the Upper River of the Mekong Delta to an island called Cù Lao Giêng. There the French nuns took charge of Mây, or should we call him Pierre for the time being, since only French was spoken in the school. As he tearfully waved goodbye to his father, the eight-year old boy realized that for the first time in his life he would be away from the farm, his brothers and sisters, his father and his mother. The distance was only a few kilometers, but the school might as well have been in a foreign country with other customs, other rules and, especially, another language, which Pierre was hearing for the first time and which was absolutely incomprehensible. For weeks, the boy cried every night as he struggled to adapt to this new environment, longing for the comfort of his mother and father. Whenever the occasion presented itself, he would run to the river's edge in the hope of seeing his father's boat coming to get him. But the boat did not come and gradually the boy became accustomed to the school. He made friends with some of the other boys from his own village. He began to understand the new language, to speak and even to read and write. He learned the secrets of the accent grave, the accent aigu and the accent circonflexe. At six o'clock every morning he attended Mass and his faith was strengthened under the tutelage of the strict but kindly nuns. It was a hard year, but a crucial one for his intellectual and spiritual development. Nevertheless he looked forward with joy to his return to his family and village at the end of the year.

When he returned, Pierre became Mây again, for he was to spend the next year at Bến Dinh, the village school. This meant another huge adaptation, for the schooling was now in Vietnamese, and although Mây was perfectly at ease in speaking his native language, learning to write was another matter. The familiar accents were still there, but they acquired new significance and were accompanied by a host of other diacritical marks. The Vietnamese writing system, called *quốc ngữ*, was devised in the early 17th century by a French Jesuit priest, Alexandre de Rhodes. Previously Chinese characters had been used, which meant that literacy was restricted to a small elite class. The *Quốc Ngữ* script, using Latin characters, only came into general use in the early 20th century but is now universal in Việt Nam. The numerous diacritical marks are necessary because Vietnamese is a tonal language: rising or falling pitch combined with differences of intensity change the meaning of individual syllables and must therefore be indicated in writing. The difficulty of learning such a system is certainly less than that of learning to read in English or French, where the relation between sound and symbol is tenuous to say the least; nevertheless learning to read and write one's own language is a major hurdle for every child. Literacy is too often taken for granted in later life as reading and writing become effortless through constant practice. Only adults who become literate in later life can measure the scope of a child's achievement in acquiring these skills in his first years of schooling.

As young Mây proceeded through elementary school, he was growing in mind and spirit and also in independence and self-reliance. Soon he was again to be separated from his family, attending a different school in another village which his father had scouted out for him. Bến Siêu was not a boarding school, so Mây stayed with his uncle, a brother of his mother. The following year he attended yet another school, Tân Quới, on an island called Cù Lao Tây (French Island), this time staying with his aunt, a sister of his father. Such examples of mutual assistance within a family are typical of Vietnamese society, where family ties are very strong.

Finally, in 1957, Mây completed his elementary schooling and returned to his family. The news was that a priest from the seminary in Sóc Trăng City, located in another province, was coming to the parish to give an entrance examination to those students who might qualify for admission to the *Minor Seminary,* the equivalent of a North American Catholic high school with emphasis on training candidates for the priesthood. Feverishly, Mây set about preparing for the examination. In all, eleven candidates presented themselves to the visiting priest. When the results of the examination were announced, it was learned that only two had passed, one of whom was Hồ Văn Mây.

Passing the examination meant that Mây could enroll in the seminary, but it did not provide any financial help. Once again his parents managed to scrape up the funds required for meeting Mây's bare necessities, both from their own meager savings and by borrowing from more fortunate relatives. Mây's mother prepared a package for the trip: a decent set of clothes, a pair of shoes and a few other essential items. But Mây began to have his doubts about this new departure. What would life in a seminary be like? He knew nothing about it, except that he would have to wash his own clothes, and this dismal prospect seemed to overshadow everything else! In truth he was very frightened by the idea of being so far from home, so completely on his own, so isolated from his brothers and sisters and his loving parents. Mây went to say goodbye to his parish priest who gave him his blessing and advised him to accept this new challenge with courage and resolve. Mây's parents offered their loving encouragement and promised they would pray for his success. Nevertheless, Mây did not sleep the night before his departure, and it was with a heavy heart that he said goodbye the next morning to his mother, his brothers and sisters and a few relatives who had come to see him off. He was in tears when he watched them fade into the distance as his father's boat set out across the river. Somewhere on the other side, Mây would board the bus for Sóc Trăng, but for the moment he watched the water slip by the side of the boat. That boat again! The boat of gloom and separation. The boat of destiny.

III. Preparations

Sóc Trăng City, where the Beatified Đoàn Công Quý Seminary was located, is a considerable distance from the area where the Hồ family lived, near the point where the lower branch of the Mekong empties into the South China Sea. The local population of Sóc Trăng is mainly of Khmer (Cambodian) origin and there are several impressive Buddhist pagodas, new and old, which tourists today visit with interest. One such pagoda was in fact under construction in the years Mây was to spend in Sóc Trăng. Another, known as the *Chùa Dơi,* or "bat pagoda", is home to a huge colony of very large bats who take wing in the evening to feed on the fruit of the surrounding orchards, a spectacle which must surely have impressed the new arrivals at the Seminary. Vestiges of the French colonial era, architectural and otherwise, are today gradually disappearing from Sóc Trăng, but at the time Mây was there, they were still very much in evidence, and this included the Seminary itself.

The Seminary was organized on the model of a French lycée, except that it was of course a private religious institution, under the direction of its Superior, Father Huỳnh Văn Mão. Instruction was in Vietnamese, but textbooks were generally in French and sometimes even in Latin. Discipline in the study halls, refectory and dormitories was maintained by the *maîtres d'internat* (familiarly known as "pions"), youths who had them- selves been students not long before, and who enjoyed exercising their new-found authority over their younger charges. If one were in their good graces, all went well, otherwise the pions could make one's life miserable indeed. Boys being boys, the youthful scholars were not above playing occasional pranks, some in doubtful taste, at the pion's expense. These usually resulted in reduced rice rations for the week. In general, however, a very strict level of discipline was maintained. An important part of each student's evaluation was the grade given for "conduite" or behaviour. Three unsatisfactory grades in this column and the student was invited to leave the Seminary. Academic evaluation was also very severe; it is not surprising that of the class of 57 pupils who began the Minor Seminary that year, only three eventually completed their studies all the way through and acceded to the priesthood.

One can only imagine with what trepidation the new arrivals began their life in the Seminary. After the opening ceremonies of the "Rentrée", during which the superiors and teachers welcomed the students and invited them to deepen their spirituality and apply themselves diligently to their studies, life in the school soon settled into a rigorous routine. A typical day began at 5:30 a.m. when the students gathered in the chapel for prayers and meditation, followed by the six o'clock Mass. After breakfast, classes began and continued until noon. In accordance with the Vietnamese custom of an extended lunchtime and rest during the hottest hours of the day, classes only resumed at two o'clock and ended at five, when the students finally had some free time. This was devoted to sports, mainly volleyball and football (soccer), or games such as chess, dominoes and cards. Dinner was at seven, followed by evening prayers at eight. Then it was time to retire to the dormitory. It can be imagined that sleep was not long in coming to the young seminarians, who knew they would be rising at five the next morning.

At least an hour of each day was devoted to the study of biblical texts, both in Latin and Vietnamese. Bilingual versions of the Old Testament (1914) and the New Testament (1916) had been published by the Société des Missions Étrangères in Paris and made available to the Vietnamese seminaries. The profound truths of the Old Testament required much explanation and interpretation on the part of the teachers, but the luminous and universal message of Divine redemption and the promise of eternal life contained in the gospels of Mát-thiêu, Mác-cô, Lu-ca and Gio-an spoke directly to the young students. The meaning of the name *Emmanuel*, *"Thiên Chúa ở cùng chúng ta"* (God is always with us) sustains the faith of Christians everywhere, and so it was to help stay the course of Hồ Văn Mây in his journey to the priesthood, through the periods of indecision, crisis and suffering he was later to endure.

Towards the end of the year the students at the Seminary began to look forward to summer vacation and returning to their families. A summer camp was also being organized and this opportunity for the boys to enjoy an outdoor adventure together was eagerly awaited by many. Mây did so want to be part of the group, but there was a major difficulty: the camp required some special clothing that he simply did not have and could not buy for lack of money. In spite of all his hard work during the year and the strict discipline to which he had been submitted, Mây would apparently be excluded from the group and denied the reward of this valuable experience. Measuring the depth of her son's disappointment, Mây's dearest mother came once again to the rescue. Most of the *piastres* she had managed to accumulate during the year through the sale of her chickens and ducks, plus a little extra contributed by her kindly brother, went toward the purchase of the necessary clothing. Mây was able to go to the camp after all! It was one more example of Phạn's constant spirit of sacrifice and love for her children in the pursuit of her dreams for their future. Mây returned to the Seminary with renewed resolve to persist in his studies in the coming years so that his mother's faith in his own destiny might be rewarded.

In 1962, the Seminary was moved from Sóc Trăng to the town of Cái Răng, near Cần Thơ, the largest city of the Mekong Delta. This was nearer to his home village and enabled Mây to see his family somewhat more frequently during the two more years that he continued towards completion of the Minor Seminary. Still, there were long periods when he was confined to the Seminary and would have given anything just be with his mother and the family for a while.

Phạn knew this and, on one occasion, arranged to pay Mây a visit. She had her own small boat which she would sometimes load up with fruit, vegetables, tobacco and other products of the farm and then, accompanied by one of her younger children, make the trip down river to towns where she could sell her produce. This time, with Mây's younger brother Đỏ as helper, she set out for Cần Thơ, where after much fatigue, they finally disposed of all their cargo. Then they pushed on to Cái Răng in the hope of seeing Mây at the Seminary. The doorkeeper, however, seeing this woman in her work-stained clothes accompanied by what appeared to be a street urchin, was of no mind to let them in. "You have no business here, woman. Now get on back to your pig sty." Phạn was about to turn away, but twelve-year old Đỏ took matters in charge. "Now look here, you, and listen good," he shouted at the startled doorkeeper. "This is my mother, and I won't have you insulting her! My brother is a boarder in this place and we've come a long way to visit him! Now you let us in!" When the doorkeeper still refused them admission, Đỏ simply upped the tone and went on even louder than before: "Let us in! Let us in! If you don't I'm gonna just stand here shouting until you do!" Phạn was trying to hush him up, but Đỏ would hear nothing of it, until finally a superior appeared to see what was causing all the ruckus. Parents did have the right of visit, he admitted, and ushered them into the parlor, where they were soon joined by a joyful Mây w.. embraced his mother. "We almost had to go away, but Đỏ insisted," said Phạn. Mây gave his brother a big hug and told him, "You just go on taking care of Mom like that and I'll love you forever!"

After two years at Cái Răng it was necessary for Mây to make another change, because the Á Thánh Quý Seminary in Cái Răng did not offer the higher classes, such as Troisième, Deuxième and Première. (The French system counts years of study down from the top, First coming after Second, after Third, and so forth.). The students who had succeeded in continuing as far as they could go at Cái Răng were then sent to Saint Joseph's Seminary (Chủng Viện Thánh Giuse) in the great city of Sài Gòn.

Sài Gòn, often described in colonial times as the "Pearl of the Orient", was and remains the largest city in Việt Nam. Almost completely destroyed in the mid-nineteenth century by a French naval bombardment, it was subsequently rebuilt on the model of a French colonial city. In the course of the twentieth century, the city developed into a huge commercial and industrial center, bearing the marks of both urban sophistication and immense human toil.

At Saint Joseph's, however, the students led a rather cloistered life, isolated from the bustle and turmoil of the metropolis outside their walls. They remained more or less unaware and unaffected by the political changes in the country and the gathering clouds of civil war. The last

French colonial troops had left South Việt Nam in 1956, following the defeat of the French forces at Điên Biên Phủ and the separation of Việt Nam into two separate states in 1954. A certain stability had been established in the South by the government of president Ngô Đình Diệm, but a coup removed president Diệm from power in 1963, the very year Mây entered Saint Joseph's, and succeeding governments suffered from corruption and the inability to deal with social unrest and hostile military pressure from the Việt Cộng in the North. As the French influence declined, American presence in South Việt Nam increased. Already a sizeable contingent of American military advisors was present in Sài Gòn and other cities, and their numbers were to increase dramatically in the years to follow. The stage was being set for the terrible conflict which was to follow.

As Mây's year at Saint Joseph's Seminary was drawing to an end, he began to measure the difficulty of continuing his studies there for another year. There was of course the question of finances. The family's resources had been stretched to the limit and the basic needs of the other children had to be taken into consideration as well. The climate of violence and political instability which was having an ever-increasing effect on daily life added to their difficulties. And then too, Mây realized he had come to a point where he needed to interrupt the life of constant study and isolation from society that he had been living. Did this mean he was putting his vocation in doubt? Mây wondered. The thought of all his parents had done for him and his mother's shining dream for his future troubled him greatly. Or was this part of some plan for his life, a chance for him to serve others for a while, a chance to give back a bit of what he himself had already received? As Mây returned home from Sài Gòn he was assailed by doubts and indecision. How many lives have known these terrible moments of soul-searching, when one's whole future seems to hang in the balance!

And then, quite unexpectedly, Mây's path seemed to straighten again. He had heard that the bishop of Long Xuyên, a city not far from Mây's own village, was in desperate need of any help he could get in maintaining his parishes. Mây set out to see Bishop Nguyễn Khắc Ngữ, who welcomed the visit of this twenty-year old seminarian who showed such strong faith and ideals. Briefly he outlined the situation to him. The coastal region of the Mekong Delta along the bay of Thailand had been the scene of violent conflicts between government forces and Việt Cộng insurgents. Now it appeared that the Việt Cộng were getting the upper hand in the region and, because of their hostility to the Church, were making conditions in the parishes extremely difficult. Many priests and other Church workers had been forced to leave, and those remaining could scarcely handle their increasing obligations. The Bishop proposed to send Mây to help Father Lương Công Đại in the beach town of Hòn Chông, not far from the Cambodian border. Mây would have a room in the rectory and assist Father Lương in all his duties. Mây readily accepted this

proposal in spite of the obvious danger and set out for
Hòn Chông.

For several months all went relatively well and,
although the situation remained extremely tense, Mây
had little time to worry about his safety and well being.
He had been assigned to teaching in the local elementary
school. There was one major problem: none of the pupils
spoke Vietnamese! The population here was mainly Han
Chinese (with some Khmer and Cham elements included)
and Chinese had become the vernacular language of the
community.   Not just any Chinese, however, but that
particular to the island of Hainan, called *Min Nan*, or
Hainanese. Because of the practice of Chinese immigrants to concentrate in certain areas according to their
ancestral Chinese province and dialect, chance had
determined that a congregation, or *bang*, of Hainanese
origin had established itself in this region. Some residents
descended from families who had arrived a hundred or
more years previously. Others had joined them more
recently. In 1950, Hainan was one of the last regions to
be abandoned to the Communists by the retreating Na-
tionalist forces, and some islanders had no doubt escaped
by sea, eventually arriving in this coastal area of the
Mekong Delta, where they had prospered because of their
work ethic and mercantile skills. Christianity was strong
among them, as Hainan had long been a sort of stepping
stone for Christian missionaries on their route toward
mainland evangelization. Mây had no choice but to set
about learning the *Min Nan* language, which he did right

in the classroom with his pupils, and was soon able to communicate effectively with the members of the Chinese community. In so doing he rapidly gained their sympathy and friendship.

Fighting between the Việt Cộng and government forces had erupted with renewed intensity. Within a short time the Việt Cộng had effectively gained control of the area. A climate of terror reigned across the land as the Việt Cộng began a purge of those elements they perceived to be contrary to their cause, notably the Church and the Chinese communities.

Now Mây began to realize the degree of his own personal danger, not knowing what might happen to him from one day to the next. One day, having been advised of a Việt Cộng raid, Mây and other members of the community managed to take a boat to a small island some fifteen kilometers off the coast, where they would remain until, they hoped, the immediate danger had passed. When they returned to the mainland, however, they found that the situation had only worsened. Every morning and evening the people were rounded up to listen to harangues by the Việt Cộng on loudspeakers in the villages. Arrests and interrogations had begun in earnest. Father Lương had simply disappeared: his fate was unknown. Manfully, Mây did his best to carry on the work of the Church, assuming all duties himself. However, it was not long before he too was brought in for interrogation.

A Communist official who had just appeared from nowhere was busy deciding the fate of anyone suspected of loyalty to the central government. Just as the Pharisees had done in Biblical times, he asked each one an apparently innocent question, hoping to trick that person into betraying his allegiance to one side or the other.

"Comrade," he said to Mây, "what can we do to have lasting peace in our country?"

For his own safety, Mây might have been advised to answer something such as: "Free our country from the imperialistic puppet government in Sài Gòn and place the Church in the service of the new state." Instead, inspired by his faith, Mây echoed the words of Christ: "Love your neighbours, even your enemies, forgive those who persecute you and pray for them." This declaration was met with cold indifference on the part of the official, but for the time being he allowed Mây to return to the community with the stern warning that he would be carefully watched.

Now Mây lived in constant fear that the official would come back to arrest him once and for all. He hid out as best he could, taking his meals with a generous and kindly Chinese family. Mây had trouble eating however, and sleep was next to impossible. He realized that his own family had no idea where he was and that he might never see them again. Meanwhile, violent confrontations continued unabated as government forces attempted unsuccessfully to regain control of the region. There were daily air raids and naval bombardments, all more or less ineffectual due to the difficulty of pinpointing military targets. For civilians however, life in this inferno was next to impossible, as they never knew where the next shell or bomb would fall. Some simply dug holes in which to take refuge, entrusting their survival to fate. The Việt Cộng, however, reinforced by arms and ammunition pouring in across the border from Cambodia, effectively strengthened their hold on the land and on the people. Many families attempted to evacuate the area, some successfully, others not. All was terror and chaos around him, yet Mây would not and could not abandon his newfound parishioners. Finally some of his Chinese friends convinced him to join them as they secretly relocated to the town of Rầy Mới, a few kilometers inland, which was somewhat less subject to the aerial and naval attacks. This was no guarantee of safety from the Việt Cộng, however, and Mây would have to remain hidden as far as possible.

At home, parish priest Trần Công Triệu had become acquainted with the situation of the Church along the coast. He informed Ngự, Mây's father, that in his opinion Mây was currently in grave danger and urged Ngự to attempt to reach Mây and bring him back to the parish. Mây's mother Phạn had also been extremely worried about the safety of her son and when Ngự told her of his plan to bring Mây home, she could only pray for the success of his mission.

Ngự set out for Hòn Chông, where many discreet inquiries finally led him to Mây's hiding place in Rầy

Mới. Father and son were joyfully reunited, but Ngự insisted that Mây leave the Chinese community and return to the relative safety of his home village. The Chinese families begged Mây to stay with them, but Mây could not disobey his father, who reasoned that a dead seminarian would not be of much use to anyone and would certainly have no hope whatever of one day becoming a priest! When Mây said goodbye to the families, there were tears all around. They embraced Mây and begged him to come back, promising they would look after him. But as Mây left with his father, he realized that it would probably be a very long time before he would be able to do so. The two travelers passed unnoticed through the countryside and soon Mây found himself once again safely in his own home in the company of his parents, brothers and sisters. Phạn drew her son to her bosom and thanked God for his return, consoling him as best she could for not having been able to carry out to the end the mission with which the Bishop had entrusted him.

Yet Mây remained despondent and began once again to question his calling to the priesthood. His faith remained strong, but he began to wonder if God had not found him unfit to continue his struggle in the face of so many obstacles. He had been obliged to interrupt his studies and had failed, or so he thought, in his active intervention in the work of the Church. For a while he tried to just not think about it, to forget everything, to not even mention the vocation his mother had dreamed about, for which his father and family had already made so many sacrifices. But in the end he could not resist the deep longing in his heart to fulfill that dream and to make his life count for something in the service of his faith. What could he do next to get back on track and advance toward that far off goal? Finally Mây decided to seek advice from his friend, Brother Nguyễn Văn Đệ, a nephew of Mây's parish priest Father Triệu, with whom Mây was much later to live perilous hours. Đệ and Mây had met when Mây was attending Minor Seminary in Sóc Trăng and Đệ was with the Lasan Taberd fraternity of the Order of Saint François de Sales in the same city. Later the two became much better friends, spending summers together with Đệ's uncle Triệu. Although their friendship was one of equals, Đệ was five years older than Mây and well on the way to the priesthood, having completed the Major Seminary. He had also spent some time with the Lazarist Community in the city of Đà Lạt. He offered to recommend Mây to that community, suggesting that if Mây was willing to go to Đà Lạt and work with the Lazarist Fathers, he could take advantage of one of the numerous educational institutions located there in order to complete the final two years of his Minor Seminary. With some misgivings, Mây decided to accept this proposition and go to Đà Lạt, where he was to spend the next two years.

Mây found Đà Lạt to be a strange and beautiful place, a sort of Shangri-la located at an altitude of 1300 meters in the central highlands of Việt Nam. Đa Lạt was at once geographically isolated yet closely bound to the great intellectual and spiritual movements of the outside world. The city had been founded in the late 19th century by Alexandre Yersin, a French doctor of Swiss origin who spent some forty years in Indochina, where he was the director of the local Pasteur Institute. He was the first to isolate the bacillus of the plague, that terrible scourge which had so ravaged the European continent during the Middle Ages and was still endemic in many parts of the world, including Southeast Asia. For his discovery Yersin is universally honored in Việt Nam; many cities still have a street bearing his name. Recognizing the healthy climate and moderate temperatures prevalent in the area Yersin had recommended that the future city of Đà Lạt be developed as a health resort and vacation center. Even before the construction of a railway from Sài Gòn to Đà Lạt in 1935, the city had attracted many French colonial residents as well as numerous Vietnamese intellectual and religious communities. Mây marveled at the beauty of the setting, so different from his native Mekong Delta. Five volcanic peaks dominate the horizon around the town, built around a magnificent lake. Orchids blossomed everywhere and the air was permeated with their delicate scent. Mây was soon able to identify the stately colonial buildings that housed the numerous religious and secular institutions of the city: the Jesuit Seminary, the Catholic University, the Adran Lasan College, the Governor General's mansion and many more. Students at the Lycée Yersin thronged boisterously to their classes, those same students who, years later, were to revive their memories of these carefree times from various places of exile in France, Switzerland, the United States and other points around the globe. The nuns of the prestigious girls' school, the Couvent des Oiseaux, shepherded their neatly attired charges through the streets on their daily *promenade*. The noisy bustle of the market place rang with the accents of French, which was everywhere to be heard. This was indeed a fascinating place, and Mây resolved to devote himself here to the work of the Lazarists and to the completion of his baccalaureate, which he had arranged to do at the Adran Lasan College. Yet he knew in his heart that this was not the place he would spend the rest of his life. He felt that God was calling him to be elsewhere. Where, he did not as yet know.

So it was that two years later, in 1967, his baccalaureate representing the completion of the Minor Seminary firmly in hand, Mây prepared to say goodbye to his friends in the Lazarist community and return to the Mekong Delta. The Brothers would have liked him to join their Order and remain in Đà Lạt, but they too realized that Mây's calling was elsewhere and wished him Godspeed on his journey. As for Mây, he did not know exactly what his next step would be. He prayed that he would soon be enlightened in that regard and indeed the answer was not long in coming.

No sooner had Mây returned home to be reunited with his family than he received a message from the Bishop of

Vĩnh Long Diocese, Bishop Nguyễn Văn Thiện. The Bishop was a former classmate of Mây's parish priest, Father Triệu, and also the former priest of Cù Lao Tây parish, where Mây had attended elementary school. Interestingly, Nguyễn Văn Thiện is today the oldest living Catholic Bishop, having recently celebrated his 100th birthday in Nice, France. At the age of 60, he was already a much respected figure in the Vietnamese Church. The Bishop had heard of Mây's success in completing the Minor Seminary in Đà Lạt and pressed Mây to now continue his studies in the Major Seminary in Vĩnh Long. Mây would be assigned to work as a librarian with the Dean of the Faculty of Philosophy and former Rector of the Major Seminary of Saint-Sulpice in Huế City, Father Trần Thái Đỉnh.

Vĩnh Long, the city situated at the point where the Upper Mekong divides into several outlets to the South China Sea was not too distant from Mây's home village and the site of one of the two Seminaries of Saint-Sulpice in Việt Nam. Mây would be able to continue his studies in this privileged environment under the direction of the Fathers of the Saint-Sulpice Congregation, who were all trained in France and sent to the far corners of the world, wherever their seminaries might be located. The Rector of the Seminary at Vĩnh Long was Father Pierre Gastine, a French priest who had been in Việt Nam for more than forty years and spoke the language fluently in both its southern and northern varieties, having lived in Hà Nội as well as in the South. Mây's own immediate superior,

Father Đinh, had obtained the degree of Doctor of Philosophy (Ph.D.) at the Sorbonne in Paris. He was equally versed in all the major oriental philosophies and even on occasion gave courses on Buddhist philosophy to visiting monks!

Studies at the Seminary were divided into two successive stages: courses of the Faculty of Philosophy took up the first three years, at which point the students moved on to another four years in the Faculty of Theology. Graduates of the Faculty of Theology would then be qualified for ordination as priests. It was a long road ahead for Mây, but at least a straight one, along which he could measure his progress year by year, with that crucial goal at the end. It would finally be the answer to his mother's prayers and his father's tireless efforts on Mây's behalf.

As the year began, Mây found himself to be one of some two hundred seminarians from three different dioceses and from the Religious Congregation of Alexandre de Rhodes, all studying in the Faculty of Philosophy. Each seminarian had his own room with a bed and desk. Mây quickly made new friends among his fellow students. and found this to be quite a congenial environment for moving forward on his chosen path.

The city of Vĩnh Long might appear to be devoid of interest to the outsider, but to Mây it was, contrary to Đà Lạt, part of his own world. The Seminary was located beside the Cathedral, about a kilometer from the river's edge and within easy walking distance to the town center.

In his free time, Mây enjoyed strolling in the town and
mixing with the inhabitants, with whom Mây felt that
particular bond of kinship which exists between fellow
countrymen whose lives are so like that of one's own
family. He particularly enjoyed chatting with those
elderly patriarchs who stationed themselves before their
door stoops, stroking their long beards and reflecting on
matters of life in general. Mây might have prolonged his
strolls along the riverfront dotted with cafés and
restaurants and presenting a fine view of the offshore
islands. These latter are today widely visited by tourists
who are enchanted by the peaceful setting, the houses
built on stilts, the tropical fruit orchards and lush
farmlands. At the time Mây was in Vĩnh Long, however,
these were places to be avoided by the seminarians, for
they were largely controlled by the Việt Cộng and an
impromptu excursion might have incurred disastrous
results for the interested party.

The smoldering war between the Việt Cộng and
government and American forces was to erupt into a
violent confrontation shortly after Mây's arrival in Vĩnh
Long. In January 1968, a sudden open attack by the Việt
Cộng at Khe Sanh was repelled at horrific cost in human
lives, only to be followed by the so-called Tết Offensive,
launched on the eve of January 31st, the Vietnamese New
Year. For a few days the Việt Cộng occupied all the
major cities of South Việt Nam. Government forces soon
regrouped however and, with the help of American
troops, drove the Việt Cộng back into hiding in the

countryside, inflicting serious damage to their numbers and equipment. This was hailed as a great victory by the military, but was in fact a psychological turning point in Việt Nam and especially in the United States, where an ever increasing portion of the population became appalled by the number of American casualties as well as the atrocities committed by their own troops. Nevertheless, the Americans continued to build up their forces in Việt Nam, increasing the number and violence of their air and land operations. In vain, churches of all religions preached peace and good will among men, but the forces at work were often greater than the power of the individual to put principles into practice.

In this climate of uncertainty and distrust, Mây tried to concentrate on pursuing his studies at the Seminary. Slowly the months and years slipped by until finally, in early 1970, Mây was able to complete the program of the Faculty of Philosophy. Now he was required to accomplish two years of pastoral service before entering the Faculty of Theology. The two years of pastoral service were to be spent helping Father Nguyễn Văn Tý, at Phước Hảo Parish in the former province of Vĩnh Bình (currently Trà Vinh Province) near the eastern coastline.

As Mây set out to join Father Tý, Mây was thinking about his progression along the road to becoming a priest. Only a few more years to go, and then Mây would be able to say, "Dearest Mother, look, your dream has come true. It hasn't been easy, but here I am, thanks to you, who planted the seed in my heart, and Father, who made it grow, and the will of God who knows all things. Now you will come to my ordination as a priest and then I will celebrate the Mass and give you Holy Communion."

But this was not to be.

At Phước Hảo Parish on the morning of October 19th 1970, Mây received the unexpected visit of his cousin, Hà Văn Thẻ, who had just arrived from the village. The boys had grown up together and were very close; in fact, as children, they had been together on that table when bandits had threatened to cut them to pieces! Mây rushed forward to greet his friend. "What news from home, cousin?" asked Mây. "Come with me, Mây," replied the cousin. "We will go into the chapel and pray. Your Mother passed away yesterday morning."

Suddenly, Mây's world wavered and congealed around him. He collapsed in his cousin's arms and completely lost consciousness. His cousin held him close for a few minutes, hardly knowing what to do. When Mây came around after a few minutes, he could only blurt out to his cousin, "You go on back to the village. I'll be there as soon as I can." Mây somehow made his way to the Seminary at Vĩnh Long where he found his good friend, Brother Nguyễn Văn Đệ. Informed of the tragedy that had befallen Mây's family, Brother Đệ did his best to comfort his friend and told him they would return immediately to the village, where Brother Đệ's uncle, Trần Công Triệu, was the parish priest. Brother Đệ immediately obtained permission to leave the Seminary with Mây. Riding Brother Đệ's motor cycle, they went

first to see Father Triệu, who asked Mây to stay a while
with him before continuing on to his home, three or four
kilometers further on. Father Triệu, knowing what a
shock Mây had received, poured a glass of wine and told
Mây to drink it. Mây did so and felt somewhat
intoxicated, as this was the first time he had ever had
anything strong to drink. Father Triệu tried to help Mây
accept his loss, but Mây was scarcely listening. When he
finally arrived home, his first sight was that of his mother
lying in the casket, her eyes still open as if in waiting for
her son. Mây approached her and, because he was the last
of her children to arrive, gently closed her eyes according
to culture and custom. Kissing her forehead, Mây spoke
to her: "Thank you, Mother, for your love, care and
sacrifices for all your children, especially me. May God
welcome you into heaven because you are truly a woman
of love. Looking up at the numb, disconsolate faces
around him, Mây added, "Pray for your beloved family,
dearest Mother in heaven. We will all miss you greatly."
In tears and wanting to be alone, Mây stepped outdoors
into the warm air. All was strangely quiet in this tropical
Garden of Gethsemane. Mây prayed: "Father, I don't
want this to be. I want my mother to be here with us as
she always has been. Nevertheless, *Nhưng xin đừng theo
ý con, mà xin theo ý Cha*: not as I will, but as Thou wilt."

It was painful for Mây to sit down everyday on the
floor in a circle with the family for meals, seeing his
mother's place empty. No one could eat properly. Mây's
younger sister missed her mother so terribly that she

refused to eat at all and wouldn't speak to anyone; Mây as well sunk into despondent silence, which he kept for many weeks. So disheartened was Mây that he couldn't imagine returning to the Seminary and the Faculty of Theology. What good was Theology, anyway? No amount of abstract reasoning could replace a mother's loving presence.

In any case, there were the two years of pastoral service to complete before returning to the Faculty. They were to be two years of action, of implication in the everyday lives of a humble people struggling to survive, to raise their families, to honour and respect those who had gone before them and somehow, by the grace of God, to prepare the way for those who would follow. There were of course betrayals, illnesses, accidents and deaths among them, but also births, nurture, compassion and new beginnings, accompanied by the renewal of that quiet strength which faith provides. Mây recognized the latter qualities easily, for they were those of his own parents: the strength and determination of his father, the love and generosity of his mother, the faith which had sustained them both.

IV. The Narrowing Path

Finally, in 1972, remembering his devotion to his mother's dream, Mây saw his way clear to rejoin the Seminary in the Faculty of Theology. All the while he would continue his commitment to practical service within the Church, this time helping Sister Nguyễn Thị Tài and her colleagues in the Order of the Lovers of the Holy Cross at the Diễm Phúc Orphanage in Vĩnh Long. Yet as Mây began this final phase of his preparation for ordination, he sensed with some foreboding that time might be running out for his country, his family and life as he had known it. The clock was indeed ticking for the Republic of South Việt Nam. The American president Richard Nixon was soon to negotiate a settlement with the Hà Nội government providing for the withdrawal of American forces from Việt Nam, leaving the weakened and demoralized South to await an inevitable onslaught from its hostile northern neighbour. As Mây completed one year, then two, then three, then almost four, the country waited in a state of frozen unreality for the final disaster to occur.

The invasion began in January 1975. Tanks, artillery and troops crossed the demilitarized zone in great numbers and began a steady progression toward the South, facing only minimal resistance. Many cities, including the paradisiacal enclave of Đà Lạt, were abandoned without a fight. A valiant last-ditch defense was finally organized around Xuân Lộc, only sixty kilometers north of Sài Gòn, but when these positions were finally overrun, the South was forced to surrender on the morning of April 30th 1975.

Việt Nam was at least now reunited after decades of political division. One can understand the reasons for commemorating the heroic sacrifice of so many lives on both sides during these horrendous years of conflict. Nevertheless, for many South Vietnamese, and particularly for the Catholic faithful, April 30th 1975 was a very black day indeed. There were mass arrests and the menace of many more to come. Anyone suspected of collaboration with the former regime, or even of a lack of opposition to it, could expect to become a victim of harsh reprisals on the part of the new authorities, including confiscation of property and forced removal to so-called "re-education" camps. Panic ensued as thousands sought to flee the country. A lucky few were able to escape by plane, sometimes under fire from the ground as they took off. Most others tried to regroup their families and live in obscurity until they too could escape by land or by sea. Over the ensuing years, hundreds of thousands were to attempt escape by boat, in fact they were to become known as the "Boat People". Almost a third perished at sea, as often as not victims of attacks by vicious pirates, who raped the women, plundered any valuables and then sank the boat with all its passengers on board. Many small craft, never intended for navigation on the high seas, were caught in tropical storms and sank without a trace. Other larger, but no less unseaworthy vessels, simply foundered under the weight of their human cargo and slipped beneath the waves, carrying all their passengers to a watery death. Even when the boats did manage to reach a foreign shore, they were often turned away and forced to continue their voyage under appalling conditions, and with even more deaths on board, before they could reach a friendly port. Of course, all passengers of boats intercepted by Vietnamese patrols were returned to the land from which they had risked everything to escape and severely punished for their attempt. Mây later heard of one group of his acquaintances whose boat was broken up on a low rock in the South China Sea. Some survivors managed to reach the rock, where they huddled together in terror and despair, as they found themselves knee-deep in water at high tide. Reported to the authorities on land by passing fishermen, they were eventually rescued by Vietnamese patrol boats, only to be subsequently interned in prison camps as illegal emigrants.

Such horrors were yet to come on that day in April when, in Vĩnh Long City, Hồ Văn Mây saw his journey to the priesthood come abruptly to a halt. Việt Cộng officials suddenly materialized from the brush to take command of the conquered land. They strode boldly into the churches, the orphanage, the rectories and the Seminary itself to announce that these properties were now in the hands of the state, their future use to be decided by the new government. In any case, activities of the Church would be severely restricted and there was to be no further ordination of priests. All Seminary records were hastily destroyed by the few remaining personnel, even as soldiers were occupying the buildings. Fearing for their very existence, most of the seminarians quickly dispersed, making their way as best they could to their home villages and farms in order to take refuge with their families.

Mây was in complete despair as he made his way home from Vĩnh Long. Here he was, only a few short months from completion of all his studies and ordination as a priest, his lifelong goal, and now all this was in shambles. Not only that, but now, if he had anything further to do with the Church, he would be in serious danger of imprisonment or worse. Well, such had been the situation for those first Christians so many centuries ago. But the strength of their faith had made it possible for them to carry on spreading the word of God no matter what. Could Mây do less? He wasn't sure that he had the courage of those stalwart disciples of another age. Would it not be wiser to forget about all that? It would certainly be safer for Mây himself and for the family. And then Mây remembered: the family, yes, the family... His father had the courage that Mây seemed to be lacking, his brothers and sisters too, each in their own way. And what about his mother who had lived her whole life with courage and generosity and was now in heaven? Mây prayed to her and to God to show him the way.

It seems that his prayers must have been answered, for Mây was soon back in the service of the Church, this time assisting his friend, the newly ordained Nguyễn Văn

Đệ, in the An Long (Phi Trường) parish of Đồng Tháp Province, near the Cambodian border.

The parishioners were quite poor, but faithful and generous with what they had and supported their priest very strongly. For the most part, these people were part of the many thousands of Cambodian citizens of Vietnamese origin forced back into Việt Nam in recent years by the repressive military regime of Cambodian president Lon Nol. The new Vietnamese government, on the eve of a full-scale invasion of Cambodia, imposed severe restrictions on these recent arrivals, suspected of possible Khmer allegiance. Needless to say, Catholics among them were subject to a double persecution. Such were the dangerous conditions prevailing in Phi Trường Parish when Mây arrived to help Father Đệ.

It would not be the first time Mây and Đệ had faced danger together. Mây recalled one incident years before when he and Đệ were spending their summer vacation with Đệ's uncle, Father Triệu. Some bandits had broken into the rectory, tied up and gagged Đệ and his uncle, and then proceeded to ransack the premises in search of any valuables. Mây happened to be upstairs and was working up his courage to go to the window and cry out an alarm when he heard one of the bandits tramping up the stairs. One glance at the swarthy individual and the pistol he was carrying (the bandits had graduated from knives to firearms) was enough to cause Mây to postpone any hasty action. As soon as the culprits had fled with their booty, Mây flung open the shutters and cried out

"Bandits! Bandits!" A throng of villagers immediately appeared, but by then the guilty parties had disappeared without a trace. Mây untied Đệ and Father Triệu, and they all counted themselves lucky to have escaped with only the loss of a few material possessions.

The sight of firearms was now nothing unusual. Việt Cộng soldiers had occupied the area and were everywhere to be seen. For the moment, they left the church alone, but both Mây and Đệ sensed that this was only temporary.

One morning Đệ said to Mây, "I don't know why you came to my room in the middle of the night and told me to take the statue of Saint Anthony down into the Sanctuary, but anyway it's done. I set it up there." Mây looked at Đệ blankly because he couldn't remember having done any such thing. In any case, he certainly had no objection to Saint Anthony being on view for the parishioners if that was what Đệ wanted, so he said nothing and the matter was forgotten.

Shortly thereafter, Father Đệ received the news he had been fearing. Việt Cộng officials informed him that since the church was now state property, it would henceforth be used to billet military personnel. Masses and other church functions would cease immediately. There was no choice but to obey and try to figure out a way to continue to serve the people without the benefit of the building.

The soldiers proved to be a rowdy lot, and there was much boasting and revelry when they moved into their new quarters. The men delighted in acts of vandalism and were soon taunting each other as to what new exploit they might perform. Telling the others to "Watch this!" two of the soldiers drew their revolvers and began to take pot shots at the statue of Saint Anthony. Given the quantity of communion wine the men had imbibed, their aim was not the best, but the two rivals finally succeeded in blowing off the head of the statue.

One can think what one may, the fact remains that these two individuals were soon to meet their own violent deaths, one by his own hand. Informed of these events, a provincial Việt Cộng official decided that the soldiers would be billeted elsewhere and the church returned to the people, if only because such incidents were embarrassing and reflected poorly on the level of discipline maintained among the troops. The statue of Saint Anthony was hastily repaired and church activities resumed, though for how long, no one knew.

Under such circumstances it was tempting to lay the blame on the Việt Cộng for any unfortunate event that might take place. But, as in any society in any time and any place, purely human dramas unfolded in which the causes can be found in the weaknesses or failings of the persons concerned. In Việt Nam, the resolution of these crises is often in the hands of the family, whose role is both to support any member in difficulty and maintain the honour of the family as a whole.

One morning as Father Đệ was walking to the church, he noticed a broken box by the side of the path. On examination, this proved to be the collection box

habitually placed at the feet of the statue of Saint
Anthony. The contents of the box had naturally been
removed, and both Đệ and Mây assumed the theft had
been committed by one of the Việt Cộng soldiers. Shortly
thereafter, Father Đệ received the visit of a parishioner,
the godmother of a teenaged girl who was active and well
liked in the parish. The woman confided to the priest that
she had an inexplicable feeling that her goddaughter had
done something wrong, possibly stolen something. This
was very worrying to her, because she loved her
goddaughter dearly and felt responsible for her moral
upbringing. Father Đệ advised the woman that if the girl
had effectively committed a theft, they should pray that
her own conscience would lead her to admit her fault and
that they should give her love and support in this difficult
confession. Making the connection with the theft of the
box, Father Đệ decided to have a talk with the girl's
grandparents about the matter. When they came to see
Father Đệ, they too felt that, although there was no proof,
it was possible that the girl had stolen the box, and if she
had, they would restore the missing funds. Father Đệ
resolved to mention the theft of the collection box in
church and ask the parishioners to pray for the person
responsible. Not long afterward, the girl's parents came
to see their priest. The father hotly denied the accusations
floating around concerning his daughter, but the mother
remained silent. With that, it was decided to drop the
matter. Some time later, the girl fell quite seriously ill
and had to be taken to the hospital. In her fever, she

confessed the theft of the box to her parents and begged their forgiveness. The girl eventually recovered and went on to lead an honorable Christian life.

Just when it seemed that the Church might be allowed after all to continue to meet the moral and spiritual needs of the Catholic faithful in Việt Nam, however difficult the conditions might be, a new crackdown was about to occur. After the end of the war, with the imposition of an American trade embargo and worsening relations with Cambodia and China, Việt Nam became quite isolated from the rest of the world, except for Communist countries such as the Soviet Union. Other influences and institutions which the country's hard-line leaders considered to be foreign to their doctrinarian outlook were to be eliminated through a program of "Vietnamisation" Among these institutions could be counted the ever-bothersome Catholic Church., whose influence was not conducive to the adequate adoration of the leaders' own secular heroes. Accordingly, all necessary measures, including police action, were to be undertaken, in order to severely reduce or entirely eliminate the Church's presence once and for all.

One morning in 1977, after the six o'clock Mass, a convoy of vehicles pulled up in front of the church. A number of police officers and an entire squadron of soldiers jumped out and rushed up to the rectory, which Mây and Father Đệ were just entering. Seizing the latter by the shoulder, the chief police officer snarled, *"Ông¹ là linh mục Đệ, phải không?* You're the priest Đệ, aren't you?"* to which Father Đệ could only reply *"Phải, tôi là linh mục Đệ.* That's right, that's who I am."

In answer to this, the burly officer unleashed a powerful blow to Đệ's upper jaw, loosening his front teeth and knocking him to his knees, where he crouched dazedly, blood dripping from his chin.

"Now get up and come with us. You are under arrest for engaging in treasonous activities against the State."

As a terror-stricken Mây stood by, powerless to intervene, soldiers brutally hauled Father Đệ to his feet, jabbed their guns in his ribs and pushed him down the path towards the convoy. A crowd of villagers, alerted by the presence of the military vehicles, had assembled in front of the rectory. Seeing their priest being taken away by the police, the crowd rushed forward to free him, pleading with the soldiers to let him go. Nothing availed however, and Father Đệ was pushed and shoved into one of the police vehicles. In a cloud of exhaust fumes, the whole convoy then disappeared down the muddy road leading away from the village, leaving behind the assembly of villagers, standing helplessly in front of the now vacant rectory.

Father Nguyễn Văn Đệ was to spend a total of fifteen years in Vietnamese prisons. Some years after Đệ's arrest, a "people's court" show trial was held in the soccer field

---

¹ ironically honorific

in the nearby town of An Long. The prisoner was made
to stand in the middle of the field, his wrists handcuffed
behind his back and a lemon in his mouth. A large crowd
of villagers from around the countryside had been
assembled on government orders, but no one could be
found among them to testify against Father Đệ, whom the
people universally esteemed. Instead, they cried out for
his release. No matter, the initial charges were simply
repeated and deemed to be approved, and Đệ was sent
back to prison. Father Đệ was finally released in 1990, a
worn and diminished man, but no less faithful to his
creed and calling.

For weeks, Mây relived the nightmare of Father Đệ's
arrest. He dared not go back to the rectory, which had
been confiscated by the authorities, nor to the church,
which it was forbidden to enter, so he took up shelter in a
miserable straw hut at the edge of the rice fields. Mây's
family supplied him with a little rice and some bananas,
the good Sisters of the parish brought him a few eggs and
vegetables, and Mây found work in the rice paddies.
Nevertheless, frequently wracked by hunger and
exhausted from the long hours of toil under the hot sun,
Mây was in near despair. He alone was responsible for
the parish now, and yet what could he do? He knew he
was under surveillance by the police and could be
arrested at any moment if he did anything suspicious. He
was moreover advised of this by three police officers
who came to interrogate him in his straw shelter. Fearing
for their own safety, the people of the parish avoided

associating or communicating with him. One day in the fields, overcome with grief and fatigue, Mây felt his hands gradually cease their repetitive movements and slump to his side. Drawing himself up and raising his face toward the leaden skies, Mây began to sob uncontrollably, his cheeks wet with tears. Gradually Mây became conscious of a human presence around him. One by one, the other workers in the field, young people for the most part, had gathered around Mây to console and comfort him. It was as if they were saying, "Come on, Mây, we all know how tough it is. But don't fail us. We're counting on you." It was a moment Mây was to remember all his life.

V. Escape

Mây gradually hardened to the work in the fields. From time to time he would meet with some of his coworkers, no more than two or three at a time, to talk about the martyrdom of Father Đệ and pray for his release. On such occasions, it was mutually agreed that if someone else, possibly a police informant, were to ask them what they were talking about, they would all say it was about conditions in the rice fields.

And indeed, the rice was planted, grew and was harvested through the constant toil of people young and old, bringing forth their life-sustaining crop from the earth and waters of the Mekong Delta. So it continues today, and rice from the Mekong fills the bowls of those who harvested it, feeds the teeming population of Sài Gòn, travels across the world to be served on tables in Melbourne, Paris, New York and a hundred other cities and towns, and even finds its way by truck and ferry to Vancouver Island and onto grocery store shelves in Victoria, British Columbia.

Mây was far from imagining that one day he too would find himself in that unknown foreign city. For the moment, his future was so clouded he could only think of going on from one day to the next. Every move he made was an extremely risky one. Although the church building continued to be off limits for the local population, it appeared that the authorities would tolerate small gatherings in a grotto behind the church where there was a statue of the Virgin Mary. As discreetly as possible, Mây would join these groups for prayers and Communion, the hosts being supplied by the Sisters who regularly made the trip to have them consecrated by Father Triệu in Mây's home parish. In this small way, the life of the Church was maintained in Phi Trường Parish. For two more years, Mây continued this tightwire existence: on the one hand, just another worker in the field, on the other, the devout servant of a clandestine Church, condemned and persecuted by the State. Finally, however, rumours began to circulate among those in the know that Mây's arrest was increasingly imminent, the authorities having become further acquainted with his previous close association with the outspoken alleged renegade Nguyễn Văn Đệ, currently in captivity, and his continued activity in the Catholic Church.

These rumours eventually reached the ears of Mây's father, Ngự, in Tân Hòa Village. Once again, Ngự felt compelled to intervene in order to attempt to ensure his son's freedom. It was evident that Mây would have to leave the country in one way or another. This would be extremely dangerous and financially very costly. Obviously, one couldn't just walk across the border into Cambodia and find immediate sanctuary in a friendly foreign country. Cambodia had recently been invaded and occupied by Vietnamese troops in the thoroughly laudable effort of putting an end to the murderous Khmer Rouge regime of Pol Pot, responsible for one of the most heinous genocides of modern times. But the Vietnamese forces were in no mood to allow this situation to permit their own citizens to leave the country. The border was tightly controlled and heavily mined. Any escape would have to be carefully planned and involve payment of bribes to innumerable officials along the way. Furthermore, once into Cambodia, the escapee would have to continue his perilous journey through that country to Thailand, where, if he were able to cross another mined and closely guarded border, he might at last find refuge.

Mây was not especially enthusiastic when he heard of his father's conviction that he must leave the country. In fact, he was terrified. He knew that he would have about one chance in ten of making it through to safe territory. He really knew nothing about Cambodia, except that a lot of it was impenetrable jungle with landmines everywhere and that it was full of soldiers, rebels and murderous fanatics who would be only too happy to torture and execute a Vietnamese runaway. Moreover, the chances were remote that he would be able to get out of Việt Nam, much less cross Cambodia and reach safety in Thailand. Large portions of even this latter country were occupied by wild rebels who knew neither honour nor discipline. Nevertheless, Mây was very much aware of his present peril, and when his brothers added their voices to his father's insistence, he began to seriously consider a plan of escape.

An influential woman in the parish and a sure friend of the Church was married to a man who had secured an

obscure administrative position in Sài Gòn. This
woman's husband would know someone who, in turn,
would know whom to approach to obtain the necessary
papers for travel within Việt Nam and how much this
would cost in the way of a bribe. Mây could then take the
bus from one point to another until he reached some area
along the border where he could enter Cambodia with a
minimum of difficulty, perhaps even with an exit permit.
All this would require a considerable sum of money, both
to bribe the official and to provide for Mây's travel
expenses, the services of a guide and further bribes along
the way. The woman estimated that at least the
equivalent of about 3,000 U.S. dollars would be
necessary, in the form of 18 karat gold tablets. Mây's
father immediately set out to scrape together this huge
sum. It would require all of his own savings as well as
very generous contributions from fortunate relatives. The
gold was finally in hand and entrusted to the parishioner
who was to accompany Mây to Sài Gòn and make all the
necessary arrangements. Mây scarcely had time to say an
emotional goodbye to his family before he found himself
on the bus to Sài Gòn. As Mây sat in the crowded vehicle
wheezing its way through the maze of rutted roads
leading to the city, he uttered a silent prayer to God,
"Lord, if you want me, you've got to protect me.
Otherwise I'm done for!"

When Mây and the parishioner arrived in Sài Gòn,
they went immediately to the woman's home, where Mây
met her husband. Together it was agreed that Mây would

spend about three weeks with his hosts while all the steps in preparation for his ultimate departure were being taken. The couple introduced Mây to a Buddhist Chinese family, originally from An Long village. One of their sons could serve as a guide to Cambodia, a country he knew well and the language of which he spoke fluently. The Chinese family made their contact with a corrupt official, and Mây, for his part, spent his time poring over maps of Việt Nam and Cambodia. At last, everything seemed to be coming together. A certain sum had been paid to the official, who had visited the couple, supplied papers and also, quite graciously, Mây thought, indicated exactly where and when he was to board the bus. Mây spent the night before his departure with the Chinese couple in order to leave early the next morning with their son as a guide.

At the appointed hour, Mây and his guide arrived at the bus station, accompanied by Mây's parishioner, who remained in charge of the finances up to the last moment. The guide went over to the counter to buy tickets. Mây sat down on a bench to wait for him.

Suddenly, Mây's worst fears materialized. He felt a heavy hand fall on his shoulder and looked around to see a police officer glowering down at him. "You're under arrest for illegal travel," growled the officer, who pulled Mây up and thrust him into the hands of his men who were standing by. The guide suddenly evaporated into the crowd, the officer went on to make other arrests among the waiting passengers and Mây was led away to an interrogation room. Where was his parishioner? Mây thought frantically. Had she too disappeared and left him to his fate?

While Mây was being held in the room, the woman was busy dickering with the police officer in an effort to obtain Mây's release. How much would it take to allow the prisoner to leave the bus station in her company? About all the gold she had on her person, mused the officer, who proceeded to have the woman searched to see what this would amount to. Apparently satisfied with the quantity of gold found, but not a bit less, the officer strode to the interrogation room, grabbed Mây by the collar and shoved him out the door toward the waiting parishioner. "Now get lost, both of you, before I change my mind. But don't worry, we know where you are, so don't try anything else."

Visibly shaken by the circumstances of his narrow escape, Mây told his parishioner it would be better for both of them if he were not to return to her house, but rather to go back to the Chinese family. The woman hailed a *xe Honda ôm*, a motorcycle taxi, which took them to the family's home where Mây would remain sequestered for several days, living in fear that the police would come at any moment to arrest him again. Now he had time to reflect on what had gone wrong with his attempted escape. Obviously someone had informed the police of his plans, most probably the obliging official who had been bribed to make the arrangements. He had no doubt been playing the game at both ends for his own profit. Now Mây was in as much danger as before and no further along in his efforts to leave the country. What's more, all of the funds that his father had raised with so much difficulty had vanished. What would his father say when Mây returned home empty handed? It was a thought that worried Mây as much as his present predicament.

Finally Mây decided the moment had come to risk the trip home. Two Sisters from his parish in An Long village had come to accompany Mây on his return. Mây thanked the Chinese family for their hospitality, and he and the Sisters slipped out of the house and caught the outgoing bus at a roadside stop. The trip home unfolded without incident. Mây soon found himself back at the point of his departure so many days before.

Briefly, Mây recounted his harrowing experiences in Sài Gòn to his family. Mây's father said nothing about the loss of the gold. It certainly wasn't Mây's fault that the money was gone, and, in fact, if it hadn't been available to bribe the police officer, Mây would be in prison at that very moment and probably for years to come. But the danger at home was even greater than before, the authorities having no doubt been informed of Mây's attempted escape. It would be extremely imprudent for Mây to stay with his family or even to be seen at all. It was decided that Mây should remain hidden day and night in a little room in a house belonging to the Sisters of Divine Providence, who would provide his meals while a new escape plan was thought out.

Mây's father was very quiet about the abortive escape and mentioned Mây's return to no one outside the family. Within the family, however, there was great concern. Mây could not remain hidden forever. He was in constant danger every day that he remained in the village. If his presence were to be discovered by the authorities, he would almost certainly be arrested. The family prayed constantly for his safety. Especially fervent prayers were said by the younger children who all loved Mây unconditionally. But prayers alone were not enough. Action was required, and Mây's father set about acquiring the funds for another, probably final, escape attempt for his son. He himself had no money left so it would be necessary to appeal once again to his relatives. These latter, after their recent generous donations, were also beginning to feel the pinch, specially so in view of the even more considerable sum Mây's father was asking. Since Mây could obviously no longer rely on public transportation, it would be necessary to engage the services of a *passeur*, a refugee smuggler, to get him out of the country and another to get him into Thailand. The total costs would probably amount to about 5,000 U.S. dollars. It was an almost impossible sum, but in the end, the money was raised. Such are the bonds that unite a Vietnamese family in adversity.

As for Mây himself, hiding out in his little room, there was little he himself could do, except wait for the next turn of events. His recent catastrophic adventure and the prospect of more and even worse trials to come had left him in a state of numb passivity. He reflected on the whole meaning of his life, sensing that it might quite possibly now be coming to an end. Was it God's intention that he meet death in some ambush or summary execution after all he had been through up to the present? The Lord must know that he had tried his best to follow His Word, in spite of all those moments of human weakness and indecision. He had tried to fulfill the mission on earth with which he had been entrusted. But had he indeed been entrusted with a mission? Perhaps his whole existence was simply a lesson in humility. *Man proposes, God disposes.* After all, why should he be spared, when so many blameless lives ended for no apparent reason? Mây thought of his innocent young brothers and sister Ren, Hóa, Hoài and Đậm who had left this earth after only a few short years. He thought of all the victims among the boat people, men, women, children, swallowed up by relentless, unforgiving seas. Most of all, Mây thought of his mother, whose loving, caring, guiltless life had ended so suddenly one morning. Mây prayed to his mother in heaven and to Mary the Mother Incarnate of all humanity to give him the courage to go on to face whatever fate might be in store for him, until such time as the Lord saw fit to end his earthly existence. Only then was Mây ready to set his mind to the immediate problem of escape and to face the reality of leaving, perhaps forever, his native land and his beloved family.

The problem of the *passeur* was partially solved when two local lads, known only as Mr.Tướng and Mr. Sồi, offered their services. The two had been operating a successful *buôn lậu* operation, trade of somewhat doubtful legality, up and down the Mekong between Việt Nam and Phnom Penh, the Cambodian capital. They had a boat with an outboard motor, spoke Cambodian fluently and were well acquainted with all the precautions necessary for making the dangerous trip. Taking a clandestine passenger would of course greatly increase the risks; nevertheless, since the bulk of their trade was in the return direction, they were willing to take Mây on board and confident they could get him into Cambodia and on as far as Phnom Penh. There he would have to make contact with another individual who, if all went well, could guide him across the country and into Thailand.

Finally, a date and a time were set for the departure. Under cover of darkness, Mây was to leave the house unnoticed and go in the company of his younger brother Đỏ to a secluded spot on the river bank where he would await the arrival of the boat. The plan was so secret that Mây could not even allow himself to say goodbye to his family. Mây did manage to see his father and his elder brother Tòa for a few minutes before continuing on with Đỏ to the predetermined rendezvous with the boat. Tearful goodbyes were exchanged and Mây charged his brothers with conveying the expression of his love and gratitude to each and every one. Would they ever see each other again? His father, his brothers and sisters, his nieces and nephews would remain here on their land, living lives of toil, honour and dignity, strong in their faith and united by their family bonds. Mây would go forth to an uncertain future: imprisonment, death or exile, he knew not which. But he promised, whatever happened to him, he would never forget them, he would always carry them in his heart, and one day, God willing, they might see each other again.

As Mây and Đỏ made their way along the river's edge, they passed near the home of one of their sisters, who lay so gravely ill that she had been given last rites. It broke Mây's heart that he would not be able to rush to her bedside to embrace and comfort her. But Mây prayed mightily and the power of prayer is not to be denied, for in time his sister did recover.

Having reached the appointed spot, Mây and Đỏ waited silently for the arrival of the boat. After a few minutes they heard the sputter of a motor, quickly silenced as the boat glided in to shore. Mây turned to embrace his brother, then held out his arms to the two shadowy figures who helped him onto the embarkation. The motor coughed into action again and the little vessel moved out and headed upriver. As Mây watched the shore recede, he suddenly had a flash of memory: the boat, the boat again. The boat that took him away to school when he was a little boy, the boat that sent him out to the Seminary and the world beyond when he was an adolescent, and now the boat that was taking him away for good. Would it be the last boat?

It was a dark night, for clouds covered the moon, and Mây was only vaguely aware of the movements of the two men in the boat. As a rift in the clouds momentarily allowed the moonlight to reach the waters, Mây caught sight of the two men's faces. Imagine his surprise to discover they were Tướng and Sồi, two of Mây's good friends in the village! Now they were to be completely responsible for Mây's safety for the next twelve days on the river as their boat slowly made its way toward Phnom Penh. They would be following the *Tiền Giang,* the upper branch of the Mekong, which would take them ultimately to the Cambodian capital, a distance of less than two hundred kilometers, but, once in Cambodia, they would only be able to make a few kilometers a day because of conditions on the river and the need for extreme precaution all along the way.

The first hurdle, and perhaps the most dangerous one, would be the passage of the border, only a few kilometers upriver from the boat's point of departure. The Vietnamese control post was located on the right hand side of the river, manned by a whole garrison of troops housed in large barracks. A patrol boat was moored nearby. The whole area was brightly lit, and a searchlight periodically swept the waters. The left hand side of the river, however, was bordered by thick vegetation and lay in darkness. The boat would have to hug this latter shore, moving very slowly and quietly. The motor was cut and the vessel glided forward in deep shadows as the two men used poles to push it ahead and keep it from running aground. Mây, dressed in his Cambodian clothing, crouched silently in the bottom of the boat and held his breath as he watched the foliage on the shore slip slowly by. After what seemed an eternity, he looked back to see the lights of the border post receding in the distance. After a time, it was deemed safe to start the motor again and the boat picked up some speed as it moved out into deeper water. For the first time in his life, Mây was no longer in his native land, but in another country, a country ravaged by famine, war and mass killings, occupied by thousands of troops of conflicting loyalties, where the danger was ten times greater than before.

When daylight came, Mây was able to see some of the cargo they were carrying. His first impression was that his friends must be in the business of exporting pineapples and bottled beverages, for there seemed to be quite a quantity of both on board. However, Mây was soon to be apprised of the true purpose of these items. All morning the little vessel steered a zigzag course from one side of the river to the other in an effort to avoid each of the numerous control points or patrol boats along the way. At last, however, it was not possible to prevent being hailed in for examination. Since they were in Cambodia, these controllers were agents of the pro-Vietnamese regime of Heng Samrin, not Vietnamese troops themselves, therefore all discussions with them would be in Khmer (Cambodian).

"Keep quiet and let us do the talking," one of Mây's friends muttered to him as they prepared to be boarded. Mây was only too happy to oblige, since his knowledge of the Khmer language was extremely limited, to say the least, whereas Tướng and Sồi were fluent speakers.

Things got off to a bad start with the controllers scowling down at the boat and barking questions to Mây's two friends at the helm. These latter assumed angelic expressions and calmly offered up what Mây assumed was some lame explanation for their presence on the river. The controllers did not appear to be entirely convinced until Tướng extracted two pineapples and a bottle of rum from under a canvas cover, and handed them over to the Cambodians, while reciting a long sentence in unctuous tones. With that, the controllers gruffly waved the boat on and the vessel resumed its slow progression upriver.

"What did you tell them?" Mây asked his two companions.

"Oh, I just said how much we appreciated their valuable work in maintaining security on the river," laughed Tướng, "and asked them if they would accept a small token of our gratitude."

"I hope there won't be too many of those," added Sồi. "We've got to make our supplies last for the whole trip."

Nevertheless, the scene did repeat itself on several occasions on the way to Phnom Penh. The payment was always the same: two pineapples and one bottle of rum. Mây now understood that this constituted a sort of highway toll, a way for the underpaid government employees to supplement their meager income without causing too much disturbance to the flow of traffic up and down the river.

Now that Mây and his companions were slowly advancing toward Phnom Penh in relative security, Mây's thoughts turned to the home he had left behind. Especially he thought of his father who had done everything within his power to ensure Mây's escape, knowing that he might never see his son again. His father would of course not know whether or not the first part of the escape plan had gone well and would be very worried for Mây's safety. Neither could Mây himself know that it was rather his father's safety that he should be worried about.

Soon after Mây's departure his sister-in-law had done some washing of various items of clothing, including one of Mây's cassocks, which she had imprudently hung up outside to dry. This was immediately spotted by one of the local police officers, and it was not long before he returned with a party of militia to search the premises, convinced that he would find Mây hiding inside. Breaking into the house in force, the men held Mây's father at gunpoint while they searched every nook and corner. Although they failed to find the subject himself, they did identify some of the possessions he left behind. Mây's father was arrested on the spot, charged with harboring a known criminal, and marched away to the local jail. There he was subjected to intense daily interrogation regarding Mây's whereabouts, but Ngư maintained a resolute silence, and all attempts to extract any information whatever proved to be vain. Finally, after two weeks of detention he was released and returned with stern warnings to his family. The family would remain under strict surveillance and their activities restricted until Mây was either located or his death confirmed. The family could now only pray that Mây was still alive and on his way to possible freedom in some foreign land beyond the reach of the Vietnamese police.

January 1980. Less than a year after being taken by Vietnamese troops, the city of Phnom Penh still lay in ruins. For the most part, the damage had been inflicted, not by the invasion itself; but rather by the Khmers Rouges during their four-year reign of terror, in a deliberate effort to destroy their own city. From his vantage point in the little boat as it approached Phnom Penh, Mây viewed the pall of smoke and dust hanging over the rubble of the once proud city. He reflected on the evil of men who do not hesitate to destroy every trace of their past and put to death huge numbers of their own compatriots, all out of blind obedience to a profane ideology.

Founded in the 14th century, Phnom Penh was, in colonial times, a pleasant city of about one hundred thousand, with wide boulevards and an intriguing mixture of ancient pagodas, stately administrative buildings and modernistic Bauhaus and art deco architecture. In the 1950's the population grew to a half million as refugees poured in from the countryside, fleeing the conflict prior to French withdrawal from Indochina. The population declined in the early 1970's when the Lon Nol government forced the repatriation of Cambodians of Vietnamese origin back into Việt Nam, only to swell again to more than a million as large numbers of persons displaced by internal strife sought refuge in the capital. Then, in 1975, the victory of the Khmers Rouges, under the leadership of a certain Pol Pot, led to the near demise of the city.

Inspired by the economic constructs of his favorite theoretician, Sorbonne-educated Khieu Samphan, Saloth Sar, alias Pol Pot, vowed to return Cambodia to a purely agrarian society through forced evacuation of the entire population of Phnom Penh. Vast numbers were marched into the countryside where they either died of famine and disease or were summarily eliminated in the mass executions so poignantly portrayed in the 1984 film "The Killing Fields". Phnom Penh was left with a population of a mere forty-five thousand, most of whom were Khmer Rouge soldiers. These latter indulged themselves in an orgy of destruction, completely gutting most of the residential areas, henceforth reduced to piles of smoldering rubble.

Mây was to spend the next month living in the boat with his friends Tưởng and Sỏi. The day after their arrival, Mây dared to venture into the city to seek out his contact

in Phnom Penh, a certain Mr. Ẩn. This Mr. Ẩn was one
of those Vietnamese Cambodians forced to return to Việt
Nam by the Lon Nol regime and who had returned to
Phnom Penh after Vietnamese troops captured the city.
Perhaps Mr. Ẩn, along with many others, owed his life to
his forced deportation, for he had escaped the terrible
wrath of the Khmers Rouges, who had exterminated
more than half of the 200,000 Vietnamese who had managed to remain in Cambodia. In any case, Mr. Ẩn would
now be in a position to help Mây along the next and most
perilous part of his journey.

As he and one of his companions set out to meet
Mr. Ẩn, Mây realized he would have to be extremely
careful in the city. Even though he was dressed in
Cambodian work clothes and deeply tanned after his
twelve days on the boat, he would have to avoid speaking
to anyone, for if he did, his lack of knowledge of the
Khmer language would betray him immediately. He
therefore took the vow of silence and relied on his friend
to guide him through the piles of rubble to the place
where he was to meet his future benefactor. As they went,
Mây was able to measure the extent of the destruction
around him. Here and there, a few larger buildings had
been spared and there were some signs of renewed
commercial activity on the street level of other half-
wrecked edifices. A number of hastily assembled
ramshackle shelters were home to some of the new
refugees who were beginning to drift back to the city
from the war-ravaged countryside. The Royal Palace and

the great Silver Pagoda remained more or less intact, but many other historical buildings and places of worship had not fared so well. The once beautiful Wat Lang Ka Pagoda had been completely destroyed and the Buddhist temple and monastery of Wat Ounalom lay half demolished, the Patriarch and many of the more than five hundred monks who lived there having fallen victim to the Khmers Rouges, who considered all religions to be enemies of the revolution. As Mây and his companion passed by one particularly imposing heap of rubble, Mây looked up to see that an entrance portal remained standing. One could still make out the chipped and defaced letters of the inscription: *Évêché de Phnom Penh.* This was all that was left of the seat of the Diocese of Phnom Penh, which had once included Mây's own home parish.

Mr. Ẩn, whom Mây had known in his home parish during the deportation, greeted Mây politely and promised to do his best to help him on his way, although he himself was unable to make the necessary arrangements. According to Mr. Ẩn, the services of a professional would be required, and he knew a man who might just fill the bill. Mây and Mr. Ẩn could meet the individual over a meal in a nearby eatery, which had just reopened, to discuss the details of the operation. Mr. Ẩn would make the preliminary contacts and inform Mây of just when and where the meeting would take place. In the meantime, Mây was to return to the boat with his friends.

Some days later, Mây received word that Mr. Ẩn had indeed set up the appointment with the person in question, who had expressed interest in the proposition, provided that the payment for his services would be up front, in gold of sufficient quality and quantity.

Mây prepared to meet the man with some misgivings. Remembering his previous experience in Saigon, Mây wondered just how far he should trust this unknown individual with the remainder of his finances. As he entered the dimly lit, smoke-filled hovel that pretended to be a restaurant, Mây's suspicions deepened. The presence of his friend Mr. Ẩn reassured Mây somewhat, but the other guest, a beady-eyed individual, short in stature but long in waistline, inspired little confidence. During the meal, the man dwelt in great length on the amount and terms of payment, but was vague as to the actual details of the operation. When questioned on this matter, he shifted his glance to another corner of the room and replied, "Just leave everything to me. We'll get you on a bus with all the necessary papers and you'll be out of here in no time." This last reference to the bus was enough to convince Mây that the man was not to be trusted, and he silently resolved to have nothing more to do with him. It would, however, be very dangerous to simply say "Thanks, but no thanks", as Mây would almost certainly be turned over to the police on the spot, so instead Mây expressed his satisfaction with the arrangements and promised to get back in contact as soon as he could put together the required payment in gold.

Later Mây informed Mr. Ẩn of his decision not to pursue matters with that particular individual, and, given the tone of their mealtime conversation, Mr. Ẩn could only agree. Another solution would have to be found.

Mr. Ẩn suggested that perhaps they needed someone in the business of refugee smuggling who could furnish proof of a certain degree of customer satisfaction as well as exact details as to how the escape would take place. Mr. Ẩn had heard of a certain Madame X, a Chinese woman who had engineered several successful escapes. He would give Mây the reference and together they could possibly come to an arrangement.

It is doubtful that Madame X had a business card, but if she had had one, it probably would have read:

Madame X
Passeuse de réfugiés en tous genres
Prix abordables
Discrétion assurée

Mme X obviously knew her business well, and when Mây told her of the previous proposal to make the trip by bus, she laughed out loud. "Even if you did manage to get on the bus, you wouldn't get much further than the first checkpoint, where you'd be arrested and shot or at least sent back to Việt Nam," she explained. "No, you'll have to travel much more inconspicuously. I'll arrange to get a guide for you, and I'll buy you each a bicycle. When you get close to the border, you'll have to leave the road and make your way through the brush to

Thailand. Nothing is guaranteed, but if you're lucky, you'll make it. There is no other way."

Mây realized there was indeed no other way. Arrangements for the transaction were completed with Mme X, two old bicycles were purchased, the guide was hired. The guide proved to be a sixteen-year old adolescent, resourceful and road-wise. Youth was no drawback. Children grew up overnight in those times and places. The boy spoke only Cambodian, therefore communications with Mây would be limited to sign language and the few expressions Mây had learned in the Khmer language: *k'nyom s'rayk dteuk* "I'm thirsty", *k'nyom klee-un* "I'm hungry", *dtou ee-naa loak?* "Where are you going?" and the universal "*Stop!*"

The time had come for Mây to say goodbye to his friends Tướng and Sồi. They too were ready to leave Phnom Penh, setting out on their return voyage to Việt Nam. The boat was loaded high with all manner of articles gleaned from the rubble and street refuse of Phnom Penh: doorknobs, lamp fixtures, window frames, anything of possible utility, plus a modest supply of rum and pineapples. Mây wondered just how they would be able to get past all the control points with this large and unusual cargo, but his two friends seemed confident enough. On the other hand, Tướng and Sồi feared neither they nor anyone else would ever see Mây again, considering all the dangers he was about to face. Army checkpoints, breakdowns, Khmer Rouge and bandit attacks, lack of food and water, sickness, the jungle,

landmines everywhere, all this gave them little hope that
Mây would make it through. All they could do was offer
hearty handshakes, wish him good luck, *chúc anh nhiều
may mắn,* and stand watching as Mây and his guide
pedaled off down the road, dodging the potholes on Karl
Marx Quay, heading for Route 5 west.

Route Nationale 5 followed the southern extremities
of the Tonle Sap, a large lake occupying the center of the
natural basin that is Cambodia. At that time of the year,
the lake was some distance to the north, but during the
monsoon season, the Tonle Sap swells to more than three
times its size, as the Mekong reverses its flow and diverts
its waters northward into the lake. Points of higher
ground along the way were often the site of ancient
temples or other shrines. A few kilometers north of
Phnom Penh lay the desecrated remains of the Nur ul-
Ihsan Mosque, which the Khmers Rouges had used as a
pig sty. A little further on, at Oudong, a former royal
capital, fields of landmines protected what was left of a
whole string of imposing Buddhist monuments. On the
northern side of the Tonle Sap, the world renowned
complex of palaces and temples known as Angkor Wat
had been preserved from destruction, having briefly
served as a residence for Pol Pot, who imagined himself
to be one of the ancient kings of Cambodia. As Route 5
turned westward towards Thailand, the terrain became
wilder and more jungle-like. To the south lay the
Cardemon and Elephant Mountains, where the Khmers
Rouges had taken refuge, to the north the equally

forbidding Dankret Range. Finally, after the towns of Battambang and Sisophon, the road reached the Thai border at Poipet, the present site of an amusement park sporting a huge neon crab, but at the time Mây was on the road, there was certainly nothing amusing about it.

Route 5 had once been a fairly decent road, but it had been ground up by the constant passage of tanks and other military vehicles and was now nothing more than a string of ruts and muddy potholes, barely passable. This did not prevent it from being clogged with traffic of all sorts: buses, trucks, bicycles, ox-carts and a flood of simple pedestrians. It seemed like all of Cambodia was on the move, as much in one direction as the other. In this time of great upheaval, people did not seem to know where they were going, only that they were going away from where they had been. The road was lined on both sides with the barracks of half-starved Vietnamese troops and every ten kilometers there was a checkpoint where bamboo poles barred the way, while Vietnamese guards boarded any and all motor vehicles and removed all suspicious passengers at gunpoint. As Mây and his guide approached the first of these checkpoints, they could hear the wails and lamentations of women and the terrified cries of children as they were herded into detention compounds beside the road. Mây and his guide, however, mingled with the crowd of foot travelers, lowered their heads, pushed their bicycles under the bamboo poles and continued their way past the checkpoint, leaving behind the savage shouts of the guards and the anguished cries of their captives. "There but for the grace of God and my own good judgment go I," thought Mây briefly, but he didn't have time for any lengthy reflections; his guide was keeping up a fiendish pace and kept motioning for Mây to catch up. Mây was in a state of complete exhaustion, his legs numb and throbbing as he pushed down again and again on the resisting pedals of his decrepit bicycle. Nevertheless, on they went, kilometer after grinding kilometer, down that road of sorrows towards the ever receding western horizon.

Mây was unsure of the names of the desolate towns they passed through: Kampong Chhnang, Pursat, Maung, Battambang. Any signs they may have seen were written in the Cambodian script and therefore incomprehensible. At that point, sweat pouring down his brow, bitten by mosquitoes and black flies, dead with exhaustion, Mây couldn't have cared less. All he knew was that they were gradually eating away the 185 kilometers that separate Phnom Penh from the Thai border. Finally they arrived in a town with the unlikely name of Sisophon, which Mây recognized as the last major agglomeration before the border, only about thirty-five kilometers further on. Here Route 5 was joined by Route 6, which skirts the northern reaches of the Tonle Sap, and the confusion of military vehicles, carts and starving foot travelers was extreme. However, few civilians ventured to travel on to the border on route 5, for here the military security was very tight and it was not possible to just show up at Poipet, say hello, and cross over into Thailand. Mây's guide signified they would have to leave the road and strike out to the north across the jungle. For a while they cycled on foot paths, but these soon gave out in the tangle of the underbrush and any further progress would have to be made on foot. It was decided they would stop and rest for a few hours before this last, and most dangerous, leg of their trip. Mây knew the area was full of mines placed in the most unlikely places and was thankful he had his guide to show him how to avoid them, or at least share the danger with him. The guide seemed confident, even jovial. He kept pointing in a certain direction and repeating "Xiam! Xiam!". What he neglected to say was that Siam, or Thailand, was more than 50 kilometers away, that they had no more food or water, that the whole area was infested with mines, mosquitoes, flies, snakes, wild animals and equally wild guerrillas of various allegiances: Khmers Rouges, or just ordinary bandits. None of that seemed to bother the guide, who made a sign to Mây that they should get some sleep. In spite of his growing hunger and thirst, Mây was so exhausted he simply stretched out on the moss-covered ground and fell asleep immediately. When he woke up a few hours later, one of the bicycles was gone. The guide was nowhere to be seen.

VI. Survival

Mây surveyed the tangle of jungle before him in the general direction the guide had pointed the evening before and could discern no sort of path. The remaining bicycle would have to stay where it was. Hunger gnawed at him, but there was nothing for any sort of breakfast, so Mây simply pushed forward into the brush in the hope of finding something he could eat. As the hot sun began to beat down on the jungle, thirst overpowered hunger. Still, there was no sign of any collected rainwater, so he could only stumble on through the bushes, their tough branches tearing at him as he went past. At one point he found a few berries, which he swallowed without caring whether they were poisonous or not. On he went, one foot before the other through swarms of flies, climbing over rocks, falling into gullies, pushing ahead, no matter what.

How long Mây kept this up he could not remember. He only knew he had to find something to drink and eat or he would soon be so weak he wouldn't have the strength to go on. Finally, as he was crossing a little clearing in the forest, he saw that some animals had perhaps been grazing there, for the soil was humid and pocked with hoof marks. A few of these even contained a little brownish liquid. This was probably more urine than rainwater; nevertheless, Mây scooped some of it up in his hand and gulped it down his parched throat, filtering out the mud and sand with his teeth. Some time later, he managed to catch two lizards sunning themselves on a rock. Twisting off their heads, Mây sucked up the blood, then gagged and very nearly vomited the awful food he had just ingested, before it settled in his stomach and gave him a little more energy to push on. At last evening came, bringing some relief from the scorching sun. At night he had to stop and get a bit of fitful sleep, for it was too dark to see the way through the jungle, but the next morning Mây staggered off again, hoping against hope he was going in the right direction. So it continued that day and the next, and the next. With each passing hour Mây felt weaker than before, in spite of the vile substances and fetid liquid he managed to force down his throat from time to time. His ankles were sore and swollen, his arms covered with bleeding scratches, his neck and face blotched with welts and boils of infected insect bites, and still he went on.

As Mây dragged himself over the top of a little ridge, he saw what appeared to be a sort of path in the small valley below. But as he headed in that direction, something didn't feel right to him underfoot. Instead of the firm footing of the forest floor, it was as if the ground had been dug up and covered over again. As he stepped forward cautiously, something caught his eye a little to the right of where he was walking and caused him to stop dead in his tracks. It was a small crater in the soil, and beside it, under a swarm of flies, the mangled, decomposing cadaver of a man lying, arms outstretched, on the upturned earth, his blood-soaked clothes identical to those Mây was wearing at that very moment. A landmine had fulfilled its purpose and taken the life of a human being. How many of those had Mây already stepped over, just missing the detonating cap? When would he hear that ominous click, followed a half-second later by an explosion of flying metal tearing into the body and ripping limb from limb? Expecting it to happen at any moment, Mây fell to all fours and, sifting the soil in front of him with his hands, crawled over to a rock protruding from the ground and leaned against it. He lay there, too sick, exhausted and terror-stricken to move another muscle, and began to pray as he had never prayed before: "Well, this is how it ends, dear God, the end of Your servant's magnificent journey to the priesthood. I didn't make it, but I tried. I do earnestly repent whatever sins I committed along the way. I'm sorry I ran away when the Việt Cộng came to Vĩnh Long, I'm sorry I lost all of Father's gold, I'm sorry I just stood there when they came and hit Father Đệ and dragged him off to prison. I'm sorry for always being so scared and scared right now of dying. But I'm ready. Please come now and take me into heaven to be with my dearest mother. Please, God."

As if in answer to his prayer, Mây was suddenly aware of the clinking of cowbells. A group of peasant men and women were leading a few head of cattle down the path towards him. Mây straightened up and grabbed a long stick lying nearby. Scratching the ground ahead of him furiously, Mây hopped, jumped, ran down to the path and, waving his arms, fell to his knees in front of the startled peasants.

"*Tôi là thầy dòng từ Việt Nam! Xin các anh chị giúp tôi! Nước Thái đâu?*" Mây cried out in his native language, forgetting he was in Cambodia. The peasants glanced uneasily at each other, completely baffled by such an incomprehensible outburst from this strange creature, whom they might have taken to be a bandit had he not been in such a pathetic state. Suddenly, Mây realized where he was, and, remembering the words of his guide, he began pointing quickly in various directions while he repeated "Xiam? Xiam? Xiam?" over and over, with as pleading a look as he could muster. Gradually the peasants' expressions softened to smiles and then to outright laughter. They motioned for Mây to come over to them; someone gave him a drink of water from a goatskin flask, another, a handful of rice, still another, a bit of fish paste. Then they gave Mây to understand that he should follow them at a safe distance, that they too were headed in the direction of the Thai border.

Again they took up the road and Mây plodded on behind as best he could. At least he knew that if he stuck closely to the path the peasants were following he would be safe from landmines. A few distant clouds hanging low in the cobalt sky portended the eventual arrival of rain, but some time was yet to elapse before the Southwest Monsoon brought its torrential downpours to inundate the forest. For the moment the sun beat down relentlessly on the landscape. The air was indeed heavy with humidity, but the only moisture that collected anywhere was on Mây's sweating brow. Mây's fatigue was so great he could barely stumble along and he finally had to sit down on a rock and rest. He couldn't remember how long he had been following these kindly people, but they didn't seem to be getting anywhere. One turn was followed by the next, a rise, then a dip, then another rise. How long would it go on? How long could *he* go on? Every aching muscle in Mây's body pleaded for an end to this agony. But as Mây looked up, he realized that he had lost sight of the group of peasants. He struggled once again to his feet and tried desperately to increase his pace so as to catch up with them. Where were they? Where had they gone? And then finally he spotted them, ahead in a clearing where they seemed to have stopped. As Mây approached, he saw that they had been joined by another group, with whom they seemed to be engaged in some discussion. Coming closer yet, Mây saw that the new arrivals appeared to be soldiers, and he dropped to the ground in the hope he had not yet been seen. The men were carrying rifles and seemed to be wearing some semblance of a uniform. Bandits? Khmers Rouges? Vietnamese troops? Anything was possible. Then Mây noticed a spot of colour emerging from the brush at the edge of the clearing: the blue plastic of a tent, partially hidden by camouflage. Mây crawled forward to get a better view. Through the open flap of the tent, Mây could see that the inner surface was draped with a large flag: horizontal red and white stripes with a wide blue stripe in the middle.

Not Vietnamese, not Cambodian, no, this was the flag of Thailand! Mây was in wonderful, free Thailand, Siam, call it what you will! Salvation at last, the end of all this torture! Mây jumped to his feet, ran towards the group and threw himself into the arms of one of the soldiers of this great, heroic country!

But instead of embracing Mây, the soldier grabbed him roughly by the collar and threw him to the ground. The other men gathered round, losing all interest in the peasants, who hastened on their way. An officer shouted something and repeated it three or four times. Getting no response from Mây, he barked an order to his men. The men yanked Mây up and set about searching his pockets, evidently to see if he was carrying anything of value. Finding nothing only increased their fury, and they began to rip off Mây's meager clothing, piece by piece, until Mây was left standing practically naked, surrounded by a ring of enraged soldiers. Spouting a steady flow of invectives, their commander grabbed hold of Mây and dragged him over to a nearby tree while one of his men went in search of a piece of rope. When Mây was securely bound to the tree, the commander thrust his flushed face to within an inch or two of Mây's startled eyes and began to mutter the only word the man seemed to know in Vietnamese: "*Vàng...*" Then, shaking Mây violently by the shoulders, he screamed the word again and again: "*Vàng! Vàng! Vàng!*" Gold, where did the man think he was hiding gold, behind his teeth? The considerable sums of gold that Mây had once possessed were now in the hands of a policeman in Sài Gòn and a Chinese lady in Phnom Penh. Mây had nothing left. The only object he might have called his own was a broken-down bicycle somewhere in a bush fifty kilometers back in the Cambodian jungle, but he didn't think this knowledge would assuage the fury of these raging maniacs.

Seeing there was no *vàng* to be had, the frustrated soldier was suddenly overtaken with a boundless fury. Seizing a bamboo cane, he began to strike Mây with all his force across the legs, arms and hands, with an occasional blow down on the head for good measure, drawing a flow of blood which matted Mây's hair. The pain was excruciating, but there was nothing Mây could do to stop this ferocious beating. One blow followed another and Mây fully expected the next to come to his neck and put an end to his misery. Nevertheless, even in his mindless rage, the soldier did not strike Mây in this part of the body, for he seemed to be wary of the Christian cross on the rosary Mây was wearing around his neck. Not that the man was a Christian himself. He simply shared the common superstition that striking any religious symbol whatever would bring about some sort of divine retribution. After a while, he tired of his useless activity and withdrew to the tent, leaving Mây, half conscious, to bake in the sun. Some time later, the soldiers came back to untie Mây, return his clothes and give him some water and a little rice. Apparently they intended to keep him alive at least. What Mây did not know was that, even though he had no gold, as long as he kept breathing, he himself had a small nominal value to the residents of this far-flung outpost. For every man, woman or child brought into one of the nearby refugee camps, the Red Cross would supply several bags of rice and other necessities to the border guards. These latter, however, were in no hurry to perform their mission of mercy, and so for some time yet, Mây was regularly stripped of his clothes, blindfolded, tied to the tree and beaten in turns by the soldiers, more for their own entertainment than in the hope of obtaining anything from the hapless prisoner. The scars of these beatings would remain with Mây for the rest of his life. The great gashes on his hands are now fine white lines, the bloody slash in his scalp even yet a deep crease.

After several days of this treatment, Mây became violently ill and slipped into a state of delirious semi-consciousness. Father Hồ's memory today is rather vague as to how exactly he was delivered into the hands of the Red Cross. Incapable of walking because of the incessant beatings, Mây had apparently been carried by two of the soldiers to the camp in order that they might collect their lot of rice and medicine. He only knows that for weeks he hung between life and death and that, in spite of the best efforts of the limited personnel, conditions in the camp could be appropriately described as sub-human. The camp at Nong Chan, to which Mây had been handed over, was actually on the Cambodian side of the Thai border. It was under the theoretical control of the

KPNLF[2], one of a patchwork of Cambodian military formations pushed to the edges of the country by the advancing Vietnamese army. The huge population of the camp was composed mostly of native Cambodian refugees who had little hope of going anywhere else. Along with their compatriots in the many camps along the border, they could only attempt to survive as best they could until the Cambodian political situation stabilized. Many ended up spending a good portion of their lives in these camps until the last one closed in 1998.

From the onset, the International Red Cross had supplied relief assistance to the refugees within the measure of their capabilities. Subsequently, the United Nations, through its various relief agencies, undertook a major international effort to manage the refugee situation in Cambodia. Relief supplies began arriving at the camps and a preliminary plan for the evacuation of some of the residents gradually evolved.

Mây had almost made it into Thailand, but not quite. Now he was in this Cambodian camp, and his fate remained uncertain. Due to his illness and extreme weakness, he had not "passed security", that is he had not been officially registered as a resident of the camp. He wasn't on anybody's list and was simply considered an "illegal intruder". Unless he could somehow manage to get into Thailand, he would almost certainly be turned

---

[2] Khmer People's National Liberation Front, controlled by Son Sann, former prime minister in the government of Prince Norodom Sihanouk, the once and future king of Cambodia.

over sooner or later to the Vietnamese and either shot or
sent back to Việt Nam. But the chances of getting into
Thailand were remote indeed, especially since Mây was
still feverishly ill, unable to even stand up. Furthermore,
the government of Thailand had begun to impose strict
regulations to curtail the flow of refugees across its
borders. Mây's date of arrival at Nong Chan was later
established as February 18th, 1980. On March 12th, a man
known for his aversion to all things Vietnamese, General
Prem Tinsulanonda, became prime minister of Thailand
and immediately decreed that, as of March 20th, no further Vietnamese arrivals were to be admitted, except
small contingents for which the United Nations had
already negotiated the evacuation. A tract of land on the
Thai side of the border was set aside to house the
Vietnamese refugees already in Thailand, joined by these
small additions. The new camp, first known as 042, then
as Northwest 9, then as the infamous NW9, would only
open a few weeks later on April 18th, 1980.

One day a delegation of United Nations' officials
arrived at Nong Chan to oversee the transfer of the group
of forty or fifty Vietnamese refugees previously approved
for evacuation to the new camp. Most of these had been
waiting six to eight months for their transfer to be
accepted. Those who had not "made the list" could only
look forward to remaining in what was ironically referred
to as their "country of first asylum". Many would not live
to know any other.

The United Nations' officer in charge of finalizing the list, a Belgian gentleman adorned with a beard worthy of the patriarchs of Vĩnh Long, had stationed himself in the vicinity of the tent where Mây was lying. In spite of his fever and weakness, Mây managed to struggle to his feet and approach the officer. Summoning up his best schoolboy French, Mây addressed the officer in that language, and the officer responded in kind. Would his name be on the list by any chance, Mây asked. No, it was not, responded the Belgian, after verification. But then, seeing the look of utter despair written on Mây's features, and his desperate physical state, The Belgian officer was suddenly moved to pity, and turning aside from others present, he handed his pen to Mây and pointed to the bottom of the list.

"Écris-moi ton nom ici," he muttered. And from then on Mây was officially part of the group of evacuees.

Some time later, buses rumbled over a makeshift bridge spanning the trenches surrounding the camp. The Red Cross nurses helped Mây and the others to climb on board, and the buses headed back across the border into Thailand. So it was that Mây found himself among the thousands of Vietnamese interned in camp NW9. For the moment, this was just an empty stretch of land, but the internees were given material to stretch over the tree branches as temporary shelter. The conditions in this new camp were worse than those Mây had previously endured. Food, water and medical supplies were woefully inadequate for the huge numbers of refugees which had

suddenly been dumped here, many of whom were
suffering from malaria and other diseases or had lost one
or more limbs in landmine explosions. Yes, Mây had
made it through Cambodia and was now in Thailand, one
step closer to eventual freedom, but for many ominous
months to come, NW9 would be his home. It all looked
very unpromising from the beginning, but Mây could not
know just how terrible this place was soon to become.

At home on the Mekong delta, Mây's father, having
had no news from his son, let himself admit that Mây had
probably died somewhere in the jungle, although he
secretly held on to the tenuous hope that Mây had
somehow survived. Ngự had already asked Father Triệu
to say a funeral Mass for his son on receiving the
pessimistic report of Tướng and Sồi when the latter
returned from Phnom Penh. Now he requested that a
second funeral Mass be said. All of the family fervently
prayed God to receive the soul of their beloved Mây, if
he had indeed departed this earth, or if by some chance
he were still alive, to give him the courage and force to
go on, and bring him home to them again some day in the
distant future.

What descended from the heavens on Camp NW9 was,
however, the torrential rain of the Southwest Monsoon.
For weeks on end, unremittingly, the deluge poured
down on the camp, turning the ground into a sea of mud.
The plastic material stretching over the supposed shelters
ripped and gave way under the weight of the water,

suddenly drenching those who had sought refuge under its cover. The bamboo poles holding up the primitive tents the inmates had themselves constructed sagged and collapsed into a mire of soaking cloth and mud. Campfire sites were inundated, and, besides, there wasn't a dry piece of wood to be found anywhere in the camp. Mosquitoes lost no time in breeding by the millions in the pools of water that formed everywhere, and their swarms made the brief moments between rains as intolerable as the downpours themselves. Other creatures of all kinds joyfully proliferated under these conditions. Armies of centipedes invaded any available space; snakes slithered along the soggy grass patches; the water rat experienced a population explosion.

In hastily assembled kitchens, relief workers laboured manfully to provide some semblance of food to the thousands of residents of the camp. Stretching their supplies to the limit, they managed to supply three small bowls of cooked rice per day to each one and a tin of fish for every dozen. Leftover grains of burnt rice were boiled in water to make a sort of tea. With this starvation diet, levels of malnutrition increased throughout the camp and further debilitated the population in their effort to endure disease and the other natural and unnatural calamities foisted upon them. These latter were truly horrific.

Security, or better said, insecurity, within the camps was in the hands of a ragged band of Thai paramilitary troops surrounding the camp. The role of these *paras*, as they were less than affectionately called, was supposedly

to protect the camp from outside incursions. Instead, in
the absence of any control or discipline, they themselves
provided the incursions. At any time of the day or night,
but more particularly at night, the gun-toting paras would
burst into the camp, raiding the food supplies and
installing a reign of terror among the residents. These
boys, for most of them were just that, young adolescents
armed with lethal weapons, these wild kids could do
anything they wanted to satisfy their own desires. Human
life meant nothing to them, and they had no hesitation in
gunning down anyone who showed the slightest sign of
resistance. Back in their encampment beyond the
trenches surrounding the camp, they must have boasted
to each other about the number of women they had
attacked, the number of unarmed bystanders they had
shot the night before. No woman in the camp, young or
old, was safe from them. Mây was witness to many of
their forays and, on one occasion, to a particularly hellish
scene which was to haunt his nightmares for the rest of
his life. Before his eyes, one of the paras had seized a
young girl and was dragging her off through the pouring
rain. Lying on the ground, unable to even stand up, Mây,
along with all the others, was unable to intervene. The
girl's mother was hanging on to her daughter, attempting
to free her from the soldier's grasp. Annoyed by this
impediment, the soldier suddenly drew his revolver and
shot the woman point-blank.

Why did these young men believe they had been
given the license to commit rape and murder with

absolute impunity? They knew they would never be on any list of "sexual offenders", or tracked down as serial killers by diligent police detectives in the disinterested pursuit of justice. They probably thought of themselves as victims of circumstance, much as the soldiers in trenches who fire their bullets into the bodies of unknown and faceless enemies. No doubt their collective mindset refused to consider the Vietnamese as human beings like themselves, thus denying them the compassion they might have shown their own compatriots. In this, they are certainly not alone. History abounds in such examples: the Germans at Auschwitz, the Japanese in the Rape of Nanking, the Americans who released atomic bombs on Hiroshima and Nagasaki, killing hundreds of thousands of innocent civilians, an act which the American president at the time said had "never caused him to lose a moment's sleep." Still one wonders about those young Thai soldiers, now no doubt respectable citizens with their own families to look after. How do they deal with their memories of the events of 1980 in Camp NW9?

Then there are the children born of those unholy unions, for biology makes no distinction between rape and affectionate procreation. They would be innocent babes, wide-eyed before the wonder of the world as they nestle in their mothers' arms, each one possessing a human soul with all the promise of a fresh new life to develop for better or worse in the years to come.

For all these, the guilty and the innocent, Mây prayed as he continued to endure his own desperate situation in the camp.

Sunday, March 5th, 2006. Victoria, British Columbia. Eleven o'clock Mass at Saint Patrick's Church, Father Peter Hồ officiating. Readings from Genesis and the First Epistle of Peter. Father Peter approaches the lectern for the reading of the Gospel according to Saint Mark (1:12-13):

And immediately the spirit drove him out into the wilderness. He was there in the wilderness forty days, tempted of Satan; and was with the wild beasts; and the angels ministered unto him.

In his sermon, Father Peter remarks that this passage of the Holy Gospel has always had a particular resonance for him. He explains that in our life, we are often with wild beasts of many sorts; sometimes these wild beasts are others, more often they are within ourselves. Nevertheless, the angels are there to minister to us in these times of crisis, for the Lord will not abandon us if our faith remains strong. Who were the angels ministering onto Hồ Văn Mây in Camp NW9? Well, certainly the more terrestrial among them were the Red Cross nurses who, in spite of the terrible conditions, helped Mây to recover from his illness and regain his strength, so that he was once again able to walk and move around. But Father Hồ is persuaded that foremost among the heavenly angels that ministered to him through those awful times was the spirit of his mother, who, in the shadow of Mary the Mother of God, continued to send her love and look after Mây as she had throughout her life on earth.

As the weeks and months wore on, conditions in the camp gradually improved. Additional relief supplies arrived; the fury of the Thai soldiers seemed to be spent. But a new menace was not long in coming. The sound of distant artillery fire indicated that Vietnamese troops were launching an all-out attack on the remnants of the opposing forces along the border. Word came that the camp at Nong Chan had been overrun and ransacked with a terrible loss of human life, and that the Army was continuing to pursue the Cambodians across the border. The disorganized Thai forces were in no position to repulse the attack, and the order was given to evacuate NW9. All the residents were hastily herded out of the camp into the nearby woods, where they huddled in terror as bombs and shells fell all around them. When the Vietnamese troops arrived in the camp, however, they contented themselves with removing all the food supplies they could lay their hands on and then withdrew to positions on the Cambodian side. Their offensive was motivated more by hunger than by the pursuit of military objectives, for, although they had plenty of bombs and bullets, their food rations were temporarily exhausted; in fact, they were worse off than the residents of the camps. When the refugees reintegrated Camp NW9, they found there was nothing left. An urgent appeal was sent to the United Nations, and emergency relief soon arrived by helicopter. Nevertheless, with the increasing risk that these border clashes would erupt into full-scale war, procedures were accelerated for the transfer of inmates to holding centers closer to the Thai capital of Bangkok. The principal holding center for Vietnamese refugees, Phanat Nikhom, located in Chanburi Province, about 110 kilometers southeast of Bangkok, was opened in July, 1980 and began receiving transfers from NW9 soon after.

When news of these impending transfers reached the camp, Mây began to see a glimmer of hope. Given the circumstances, he performed what would seem to be an almost impossible feat. Borrowing a pen, a sheet of paper and an envelope from a more fortunate friend, Mây wrote a letter addressed to the Apostolic Nunciature, the Vatican's equivalent of an embassy, in Bangkok. In the letter, Mây described his situation, his ambition to become a priest and his desire to reach a country of refuge where he might complete the requirements for ordination. In his enthusiasm, Mây even asked that a Bible be sent to him, along with a collection of liturgical works, which he enumerated in some detail. He also hinted rather pointedly that an immediate financial assistance would be most welcome.

Mây handed in his letter to the United Nations authority in the camp and prayed that somehow it might reach its destination. Incredibly, the letter did arrive about a month later and Mây eventually received a reply from the

Nunciature's chargé d'affaires in Bangkok, Msgr. Thomas Yeh Sheng-Nan. The good man informed Mây that he would propose to the Italian embassy that Mây be granted a visa so that he might come to Rome to complete his studies and be ordained as a priest. Msgr. Thomas questioned the advisability of transporting large quantities of books from camp to camp, but did promise to send a Bible in the language of Mây's choice. Furthermore, in answer to the urgent plea for funds, he wrote that he was enclosing a cheque in the amount of 2000 bahts[3], although sending money through the mail was an uncertain matter. In this he was quite right, for the letter had been opened and there was no sign of a cheque. Even if there had been one, Mây would not have been able to cash it, as the corner bank had not yet opened in NW9. No matter, Mây could scarcely contain his joy at the prospect of such an imminent resolution of all his problems.

However, about a month later, Mây received a second missive from the Nunciature, explaining that Mây would be better advised to make his application to Canada and that the Apostolic Pro-Nuncio in Canada, Msgr. Angelo Palmas, had been informed of this; therefore, procedures for obtaining an Italian visa had been put on hold.

With each arrival of buses from Phanat Nikhom, a list of names was read out in fluent Vietnamese over loudspeakers. Mây listened attentively for his own, but

---

[3] about 100 U.S.$ at the time.

each time, as the H's were exhausted and the speaker passed on to the innumerable *Nguyễn*, Mây's shoulders slumped, and he resigned himself to a few more weeks in NW9.

The weeks stretched into months. The wretched Southwest Monsoon came to an end, which would have made life in the camp more tolerable were it not for the interminable waiting. Transfer to Phanat Nikhom would mean finally achieving "refugee status" and eligibility for emigration to another country, so Phanat Nikhom became a sort of earthly paradise, or at least a thoroughly acceptable purgatory, in the minds of the detainees of NW9. Mây shared the wait with the thousands of his countrymen and women whose experience had paralleled his own: the march across Cambodia, the famine, the disease, the landmines, the violence, the alternation of hope and despair. Mây made some surprising discoveries among them. Here was none other than the boy who was to have been Mây's guide in Saigon at the time of his first attempted escape. Here were a few of the former seminarians of Cái Răng, Vĩnh Long, Huế, Sài Gòn and other places, a group of twenty-three in all. Mây was their dean, the eldest among them, for he had been on the point of completing his studies when the seminaries were closed. A special bond developed between the members of this group, who eventually went on their separate ways to a variety of careers and livelihoods in different countries; one of them is known to have become a priest in Ottawa.

In November, 1980, having heard nothing from the Canadian Pro-Nuncio, Mây wrote directly to Msgr. Palmas, who had previously been the Vatican representative in Sài Gòn. Once again his letter arrived miraculously at its destination. In early December, Mây received Msgr. Palmas' reply. The Pro-Nuncio indicated that, if Mây intended to become a priest, the Nunciature would present an application to a Canadian Bishop who could patronize Mây's coming to Canada and his theological studies.

January 3, 1981 marked the anniversary of Mây's departure from Việt Nam: one year, most of it spent in these border camps. A few days later, the buses from Phanat Nikhom made their usual appearance. Again, the list was read out loud and clear down through the H's to... Hồ Văn Mây! A thrill passed through Mây's whole body; he couldn't believe his ears. "Stop!" he cried out. "Go back, what was that you said?" But the man was already into the Nguyễns and kept droning on as Mây sank to his knees.in disbelief. But yes, he had heard correctly. This time, it was the right time! Mây was on his way to Phanat Nikhom, to safety, to official refugee status, to a new life in another country. He had made it through! God had spared him from death for a reason, he was sure. He would go on to become a priest, ministering to an unknown population in some far corner of the world. But he would never, never abandon his own people, on the delta of the Mekong River, in a country called Việt Nam!

VII. Prospects

Phanat Nikhom was certainly no paradise, but conditions here were several notches above those of the border camps. True, this was essentially a prison, surrounded by barbed wire and wooden guard towers. On the other hand, food and water supplies were adequate, and the prisoners were given the opportunity to procure clean clothes to replace the tattered remnants of their former garments. The population of Phanat Nikhom already numbered in the thousands: Vietnamese, Cambodians and Laotians from the border camps as well as many of the "boat people" whose frail vessels had run aground on Thai beaches after weeks of drifting in the Gulf of Siam. The camp was laid out much like a small city: Temporary tin-roofed shacks made of plywood and cardboard lined streets and alleys bearing the names of hoped-for destinations: California Street, Texas Road, New York Boulevard. More permanent buildings housed warehouses, offices, canteens, medical clinics, postal outlets and even classrooms, where the inmates could study the language of the country to which they hoped to emigrate.

Here the new arrivals learned they still did not have official refugee status; that would depend on the goodwill of embassies of the various receiving nations located in Bangkok.[4] Applications sometimes took years to be

---

[4] Hồ Văn Mây eventually received acceptance from several dioceses within the United States Catholic Conference, including Jacksonville (Florida), Toledo (Ohio) and San José (California).

processed. For the time being, residents were simply classified as "accepted", given a sign with a number and told to hold it in front of them while they had their picture taken. They then received a pre-stamped postal envelope, that they might signify their existence to the outside world. Mây lost no time in writing a letter to his family, his first chance of communicating with them since his departure. The letter was a simple one: he was alive and well in a camp in Thailand; he would hopefully write again soon from another place; he sent his love and respects to all. Mây knew he could not write about his experiences and status as freely as he would have liked. His letter would take almost six months to reach its destination, after having been scrutinized at great length by the Vietnamese censors.

Other residents, who had the good fortune to already have relatives in the countries of refuge, received money and packages from their future hosts. A generous acquaintance of Mây with relatives in Oklahoma offered to share his booty with his friend. Mây received an elegant American-style polo shirt to complement the shorts a kindly soul had stitched for him when he was in NW9, as well as the first footwear Mây had worn since leaving Việt Nam: a pair of slippers so comfortable they are still doing duty in Saint Patrick's rectory!

The residents of the camp experienced diverse emotions. At times some hopeful emigrants saw their future through rose-coloured glasses, as if all would be calm and perfection once they got to wherever it was they were going. On the other hand, although the process of acceptance by another country was underway, it always seemed to proceed at a snail's pace, with innumerable delays and disappointments. In moments of discouragement, each refugee thought about the family, the friends and the life he or she had left behind. For many of those who had lost cherished loved ones and had themselves endured tremendous physical hardships, the future could only seem obscure and daunting.

Classed as undesirables in their home countries, waiting interminably in this camp, they may have felt that they were unwanted in the world at large.

It was to refugees such as these that Pope John Paul II addressed the following message of hope when he visited Phanat Nikhom a few years later[5]:

We are truly brothers and sisters, members of the same human family, sons and daughters of the same loving Father. I wish to share with you your sufferings, your hardships, your pain, so that you may know that someone cares for you, sympathizes with your plight, and works to help you find relief, comfort and a reason for hope.

Have faith in yourselves. Never forget your identity as free people who have a rightful place in this world. Never lose your personality as a people! Remain firmly rooted in your respective cultures, from which

---

[5] Friday, May 11th, 1984

the world can learn much and come to appreciate you in your uniqueness.

Have hope in the future. Our world is in full development. It needs you and your contributions. Take every opportunity offered you to study a language and perfect a skill, in order to be able to adapt socially to the country which will open its doors to you and be enriched by your presence.

To the Catholics among you I wish to say a special word: God never said that suffering is a good thing in itself; but he taught us through his Son, our Lord Jesus Christ, who suffered and died for our sins, that our sufferings, when joined to those of Christ, have value for the salvation of the world. Jesus Christ, the Son of God, who rose on the third day, is the foundation of our hope, now and in the future.

From Phanat Nikhom, the refugees went out to the far corners of the world, to France, Italy, England and Australia, to Canada and, in large numbers, to the United States. They opened restaurants, operated convenience stores, ran service stations, became teachers, doctors, computer engineers. They founded families and bore children to carry on in their footsteps. And, overcoming the memory of their suffering, as well as the difficulties which immigrants face in all walks of life, they have indeed made immeasurable contributions to the societies of those countries that opened their doors to them.

When Mây heard that a delegation of nuns from Quebec, Canada, was visiting the camp, he rushed to meet them. Although the nuns were not informed of the progress of Mây's file through the innumerable channels of refugee applications, they were able to give him an idea of the country awaiting him. Mây had some difficulty understanding their unfamiliar accent; nevertheless, the fact that French was spoken in Canada reassured him. He would be able to take up his study of the language where the French Soeurs de la Providence of Cù Lao Giêng had left off so many years ago. Mây would again be Pierre. That had been his name when he was in the first grade! Mây also learned that Canada was not exactly a tropical country, in fact in winter there was an abundance of *tuyết*, that white fluff which was sometimes spotted on the slopes of mountains in the northernmost corner of Việt Nam. Furthermore, although Mây might feel quite at home in the heat of July, in January he would definitely need something more than the shorts and polo shirt in which he was currently clothed.

As it turned out, Mây would have no immediate need of snow boots and ear-muffs. For five more months, Mây languished in the camp at Phanat Nikhom. Every morning he rushed to the bulletin board to see if his name was listed in the departure column. Nothing. Then, one day in early June, there it was. The formalities had been completed. Mây had been accepted as a refugee by the Canadian government and his air transportation to Canada would be provided by the United Nations' refugee agency. About a week later, Mây took leave of Phanat Nikhom, and along with a group of others shepherded by a UN official, boarded the bus which was to take them past the guard towers, beyond the barbed wire fence and out into the open country on the road north to Bangkok. After a few days spent in the airport enclave of Lumpini, the group assembled at Don Muang International Air Terminal for boarding one of the planes chartered by the United Nations for the transportation of refugees.

As the plane took off from the runway and climbed towards the clouds, Mây looked down through the mist at the rapidly diminishing green patchwork below. How quickly the whole known world faded from existence, giving way to this little enclosure with its blinking lights and muffled conversations. Somewhere down there was the jungle Mây had struggled across, the camps where he had spent an eternity. And somewhere over the horizon, beyond the wingtip of the plane, the Mekong was snaking its way down to the delta where men and women laboured in fields. How vast the world is when you live in it; how insignificant it becomes when you see it disappearing through the window of an airplane! And then, in a flash, it's gone completely as the plane rises above the clouds, under the mottled white cover of which lie a multitude of other never-to-be-known worlds. For a few hours, the whole of humanity is reduced to the person in the next seat and a few other heads and shoulders in close proximity, until, suddenly, another teeming universe, blissfully ignorant of the preceding one, bursts into full bloom and engulfs the traveler in its own self-important existence.

The traveler leaving Thailand for Canada might just as well go east as west. In the event, Mây's plane was taking the western route, headed for Paris, the City of Light, an almost mythical Mecca for many Vietnamese. It would be a long haul without stopovers, stretching the limits of the plane's range. Antoine de Saint-Exupéry was the first to try it in the other direction in the 1930's. He ended up wandering in the Libyan desert for days[6]. Mây hoped aviation had made some progress since then, as he did not relish the thought of crossing a desert on foot to add to his experiences in the Cambodian jungle. Fortunately, they seemed to be experiencing no difficulties, and the plane flew on over mountains and plains, crossing seas and oceans with a positively startling lack of concern for these obstacles. Between meals and naps, Mây spent the time chatting with the passenger in the seat beside him, a Laotian doctor who spoke fluent Vietnamese. They exchanged their experiences as refugees and discovered they had a common destination: Montreal, Quebec, Canada. The doctor and the aspiring priest wondered together what the future would hold for them in that strange city. The doctor was of the opinion that he would soon be able to put his skills to use in the new environment, given that humanity was the same the

---

[6] recounted in *Wind, Sand and Stars* (1939)

world over: the same bones, bodies and bladders. "…and the same souls and spirits," Mây thought to himself, and suddenly felt a new surge of confidence in the ultimate successful conclusion of his long journey to the priesthood.

Finally it was announced that the plane would soon be landing at Charles de Gaulle Airfield, near the French capital. Mây had only two hours between planes, so his sojourn in the land of *liberté*, *égalité* and *fraternité* was brief. Mây reflected that up to now he hadn't seen very much liberty or equality in his life. On the other hand, he had known countless examples of fraternity, within the family, within the Church and also simply between human beings. He remembered, among so many others, his Chinese parishioners in Hòn Chông, his good friends Tưởng and Sòi, the compassionate peasants in the Cambodian jungle, the bearded Belgian, the man who procured quinine in the camp to cure Mây's malaria, the woman who sewed his pants, the fellow inmate who shared his new clothes… Although Mây had also witnessed some startling examples of human cruelty and insensitivity, the acts of kindness and compassion should be weighed in the balance in any judgment of the human race. These profundities were suddenly interrupted by the crackling of a loudspeaker:

Air Canada annonce le départ du Vol 505 à destination de Montréal. Les passagers sont priés de monter à bord de l'appareil…

VIII. Way Stations

Mây's plane touched down at Mirabel International Airport, north of Montreal, in the afternoon of June 22nd, 1981. There he was taken in charge by the Canadian immigration authorities, to whom he presented the paper he had been given in Bangkok in lieu of a passport. He was given a bus ticket to Montreal, the address of an economy hotel in the city centre where his room and board would be covered by the Canadian government for a period of two weeks and funds for incidental expenses in the amount of... three dollars! Mây promised not to spend it all in one place, and he kept his word. There were a few cents left after he paid the postage on a letter to his family in Việt Nam, a letter he composed that very evening in the hotel room he shared with the Laotian doctor.

The next morning, letter in hand, Mây stepped out of his hotel in search of the post office. The warm summer air which greeted him seemed to belie the nuns' dire warnings concerning the rigours of the Canadian climate. It took Mây a moment to fully apprehend his surroundings. So this was Montreal, a city of which Mây had only recently learned the existence! It was said that there were three million people living in or around the city, but Mây wondered where they all were as he strolled down the Rue de la Montagne, seemingly devoid of pedestrians. There were no street-side food stalls, no bicycles, no sputtering *xe Honda ôm* whizzing around corners. On the other hand, there were plenty of automobiles parked along the curb and quite a few in the street as well, circling slowly like birds of prey in search of a space to rest. The Rue Sainte-Catherine, where the mammoth old post office was located, proved to be more animated, with respectable crowds moving in one direction or the other, into and out of all manner of shops, stores and restaurants. Perhaps good Saint Catherine of Siena, who lived in the 15th century and was certainly no recluse, would not have objected to her name being given to this very worldly commercial avenue. In any case, she was in good company, for many other saints of the Church had their own streets here in Montreal. Mây had seen them on his pocket map of the city: Saint-Laurent, Saint-Denis, Saint-Hubert, Saint-André, Saint-François-Xavier, they were all there. Others had given their names to hospitals: Saint-Luc, Sainte-Justine, Sainte-Jeanne-d'Arc. During his stay in Montréal, Mây would have occasion to admire many monuments of the city's Catholic heritage, nestled among the high-rises and commercial establishments, untouched by war or destruction: the Basilique de Notre-Dame, the Cathédrale Marie-Reine-du-Monde, and over on the other side of Mont-Royal, the impressive Oratoire Saint-Joseph. Among these latter institutions was the Grand Séminaire de Montréal, the address of which Mây had written on the back of his identity photo from Phanat Nikhom along with a telephone number. Here he expected to find his contact and meet his sponsor in Canada.

Returning to the hotel after his brief excursion, Mây found that Canadian immigration representatives were busy interviewing the new arrivals. The Laotian doctor had already passed his turn and discovered to his chagrin that, in spite of his previously acquired credentials, he would not be able to begin practising immediately. Instead, he would be required to recommence a part of his studies in order to meet the requirements for Canadian accreditation in the Province of Quebec. Hearing this, Mây began to worry about his own situation. He had been within an inch of completing his Theology program when the Việt Cộng put a stop to everything on that day in 1975. Six years had passed since then, six years spent in the service of the Church and the struggle to survive. Would he too have to start all over again?

When Mây's turn came, the immigration officers set the matter down for him in plain terms. The Government would continue to pay his expenses if Mây began actively seeking gainful employment, in whatever field, at which point he would be responsible for his own welfare. "What sort of employment?" inquired Mây uneasily. "Any sort," came the reply, "…factory worker, cook, salesman, taxi driver…" Mây answered that although he certainly had great respect for all these fields of endeavour, his personal ambition was to become a Catholic priest and that this was in fact the reason for his being a refugee from his home country. "If that is the case," explained one of the officers firmly but politely, "arrangements must be made to have you taken in charge immediately by the local diocese of the Catholic Church.

As soon as this is accomplished, the responsibility of the Canadian government will be considered to be at an end." Mây's file would be forwarded to the Diocese of Montreal and ultimately to the attention of Archbishop Paul Grégoire.

A few days later, some priests from the Grand Séminaire came to see Mây at his hotel. They welcomed him heartily to Canada and to the Diocese. They informed him that someone would come to pick him up and take him to the Séminaire as soon temporary lodging could be arranged. Space in the Séminaire would become available shortly because July and August were vacation months and most of the seminarians were spending this time with their families. Of course, in September other arrangements would have to be made.

And so it was that within a few more days, one of the priests returned to take Mây to the Séminaire. Mây said goodbye to his Laotian friend, who, courageously resigned to his fate, had already begun the study of Canadian medical requirements. Mây and his guide stepped out of this hotel, Mây's first residence in Canada and hailed a Checker Yellow Cab. A short drive along Sherbrooke Avenue brought them to the grand old Séminaire, a rambling assemblage of grey stone buildings located on extensive grounds just off the Avenue. Mây was shown to his room, acquainted with the hours at which the refectory would be serving meals and advised to go to the Saint Vincent de Paul Charity Outlet to acquire some appropriate clothing. Then he was left to his own devices.

With nothing else to do, Mây decided to undertake the clothing expedition without further delay. He left the grounds of the Séminaire and made his way once again into the heart of the Centre-Ville, this time on foot. In the Charity outlet, he was offered a choice of worn, oddly tailored articles, a pair of pants two sizes too large, a jacket two sizes too small. When he returned to his room, he attired himself in the newly acquired haberdashery and had a look in the mirror. One glance was sufficient to make him take the clothes off immediately and stuff them into a bag in a corner of the closet. Then he put his old clothes back on and slumped down on his cot, overcome with a feeling of solitude and discouragement. Yes, he was homesick too. What was he doing all alone in this cold, foreign city? If only he had someone to share his experiences, one of his brothers, or Tưởng and Sồi, or even the Laotian doctor at the hotel. He hadn't been given any program of activities at the Séminaire, just his room and board, and that was only until September. What then? Maybe he should have accepted the advice of the immigration officer and gotten a job as a cook or a taxi driver. Well, not a taxi driver, he'd never driven a car, but something else. But then his lifelong ambition was to become a priest. Was there no way this could ever happen?

Mây was awakened from these dark thoughts by a vigorous rap on his door. He opened cautiously and was greeted by an outstretched hand and a broad smile.

"Bonjour, Pierre! Bienvenue au Canada!"

The newcomer identified himself as Father Guy Merveille, a priest of Belgian extraction and Mây's personal sponsor in Canada. True to his name, Father Guy was indeed a marvelous man. He had been a long-time priest at Sacred Heart Parish in Victoria, on the other side of the continent, but had been called to the East to serve as a priest at the Hôpital psychiatrique de Montréal, where his immense qualities of kindness, understanding and generosity were much appreciated. Mây was not the first Vietnamese refugee to benefit from his sponsorship; there had been several in previous years during Father Guy's tenure in Victoria, so that he was well aware of the problems, both material and psychological, facing these new arrivals. He had greatly assisted them in their adaptation to Canadian life and had himself come to appreciate their resilience, their spirituality and their attachment to family and country. Most of all, Father Guy had the ability to relate to each individual, to be a friend and to make the other feel welcome as a friend.

Mây soon felt at ease with his sponsor as they chatted about their previous experiences. The doubts and feelings of solitude in which Mây had been plunged only moments before began to dissipate as the warmth of Father Guy's greeting and the interest he was showing in Mây's past and present situation took their effect.

Their encounters continued on an almost daily basis, for Father Guy was not one to just say hello and then disappear into the woods. As they continued to talk about the future and what it meant to be a priest, Mây's resolve returned and was strengthened. What had he been thinking? Adversity, as Father Guy explained, was just part of the plan.

Mây had already known many adverse situations and had surmounted them and come to benefit from them. He would persist, and with the help of God and in the fellowship of human beings such as Father Guy Merveille, he would, no matter what, eventually achieve his goal. Mây had only known two Belgians in the course of his existence. The first had saved his life in the camp at Nong Chan; the second was now saving his vocation as a priest. Mây felt an enormous debt of gratitude to that little country across the ocean which had sent two of its sons to rescue him at these critical moments in his life.

Father Guy knew that mere moral support was not enough. Even those following the noblest calling live in a physical world with physical needs, which, if they are not at least partially met, can undermine the confidence of the most resolute of pilgrims. When Guy asked Mây if he had any other clothes than those he was wearing, Mây went to his closet and hauled out the miserable collection he had acquired at the charity outlet. Father Guy opined that, although these items certainly had variety and character, they also had one important failing: they didn't fit. He stood up and went towards the door. *"Viens avec moi, on va te trouver des fringues."* Mây followed dutifully behind, not knowing whether the "fringues" in question was something you ate or just set on your dressing table to admire. What Father Guy meant was that he was going to get Mây a decent set of clothes, which they proceeded to acquire in one of the stores on Saint Catherine Street. To these were added a robust pair of solid leather shoes, as Father Guy was of the opinion that the sandals Mây was wearing might eventually require replacement as the seasons advanced. When these purchases had been completed, Father Guy suggested they forego the pleasure of another meal in the seminary refectory, and try one of the nearby restaurants instead. Mây's last real restaurant meal had been in Phnom Penh, one that he had not greatly enjoyed. Since then he had been kept alive by canteens, cafeterias, dining halls and his own pluck. This was definitely an occasion then, and one that Mây greatly appreciated. When they returned to the Séminaire, as Father Guy was taking his leave, Mây turned to his friend, grasped his hand and uttered a heartfelt "Merci, merci pour tout."

The full heat of the summer season fell upon the city as the weeks advanced, making conditions rival those along the Mekong. However, as if to mitigate the pleasure Mây might have derived from spending an enjoyably warm summer in Montreal, a new affliction manifested itself. A strange and painful rash broke out on Mây's hands and soon spread to his wrists and arms. Was it some bug from the Cambodian jungle that had bid its time before coming into the open, or the result of Mây's recent nervous stress, or simply one of those ills travelers invariably acquire on arriving in a new country or climate? In any case, it was making Mây's existence exceedingly uncomfortable. An ointment purchased in a pharmacy failed to even slightly alleviate the condition, and Mây began to wonder if he might not be required to finish his career in a leper colony or in Father Guy's psychiatric ward. Called into consultation, Father Guy simply said "Aha!" and picked up the telephone. He must have encountered the condition among his previous Vietnamese charges in Victoria, for his call was directed to a chemist he knew in that city. What was the name of that preparation which had proved so effective in removing tropical rashes? This information in hand, Father Guy proceeded to entrust the confection of the mysterious substance to a local apothecary, and Mây was soon in possession of the supposed miracle balm. Father Guy muttered a few ominous words to the effect that Mây should "spread it on and stick it out" and Mây obeyed on the spot. The yell of pain which ensued propelled Father Guy towards the doorway, through which he hastened to make his retreat, calling out over his shoulder *"Trois jours! Trois jours!"* as he went out. So, for three days Mây endured a cure more painful than the condition it was meant to alleviate. However, at the end of this period, the vanquished bug apparently gave up the fight, and the rash disappeared completely overnight. Mây could breathe a sigh of relief and consider his future more calmly.

As September approached, preparations were underway at the Séminaire for the "Rentrée", a word Mây remembered from his days in Sóc Trăng. The seminarians would soon be returning to take possession of their lodgings. Mây could of course join them, become one of their number. When Mây mentioned this possibility to Father Guy, however, the reaction was less than enthusiastic: *"Ils vont te faire tout recommencer,"* Start all over again? What about Mây's six and a half years in philosophy and theology at Saint Sulpice Seminary in Vĩnh Long, where he had received the very best training from his teachers, who were both learned and devout? Surely that was worth something! Father Guy agreed entirely, and hinted he had another plan for Mây's future, one that would lead to a priesthood worth its salt just as surely as being shut up indefinitely in the Grand Séminaire de Montréal. But patience would be required. What Mây needed now, more than a repetition of his theology courses, was a better knowledge of the language and culture of his future parishioners, the prism through which he could share their cares and sufferings, experience their joys and attend to their spiritual needs. Father Guy suggested that Mây should spend the coming year here in Montréal. He could lodge with the Fathers of the Fraternité Sacerdotale and attend classes in the city to improve his language skills. It would mean living through a Montreal winter, and that would require fortitude, but it would also steel Mây to the rigours of the Canadian climate. After that, Father Guy intimated that he had another, more clement destination in mind.

The Fathers of the Fraternité Sacerdotale were housed in a modest building on Claremont Street in the district of Westmount, a largely English-speaking enclave just to the west. Westmount might have borne some vague resemblance to Đà Lạt in that it seemed to exist on its own, as blissfully removed from the world around it as could be managed within the metropolis. In reality it was a very different place, lacking the animation and *joie de vivre* so much in evidence in the Vietnamese city. It did, however, provide surroundings where Mây might begin to be acquainted with this new language, English, and within easy access of the Centre-Ville where Mây would be taking his French classes. Languages in contact were nothing new to Mây, who had experienced first-hand the Khmer and Chinese presence in Việt Nam, and he felt he would be able to cope with this challenge.

The Fathers welcomed Mây to their Fraternity, and Mây soon made friends among them, of whom one in particular, Father Hàm, a Vietnamese priest attached to this community, helped Mây to make the transition to his new surroundings. The greatest comfort and reassurance, however, came from a letter Mây received shortly after his arrival at the Fraternity. There it was one day when Mây came back to the Fraternity after a day's activities with Father Guy. A plain brown envelope addressed in a familiar hand, plastered with a large stamp bearing the portrait of some less than venerated individual and bearing the postmark Tân Hòa, Đồng Tháp, Việt Nam. The first news from home! Mây had of course written several letters, not as many as he would have liked though, as he knew his father would have to pay for each letter received. Otherwise, the envelope went back into the mailman's pouch and was returned to the post office as "undeliverable"! In his letters, Mây had never written anything about his physical sufferings as a refugee, leaving that to the imagination of his father and members of the family. They must have guessed what trials he had endured. Mây's father wrote of his joy in knowing his son had safely reached a new country and added that the whole family would be praying for him as he progressed toward his goal of reaching the priesthood, thus fulfilling his own aspirations as well as those of his parents. Ngụ very simply stated that his whole life was now concentrated in the destiny of his sons and daughters; he had decided not to remarry, and Mây occupied a privileged place in his heart. There followed a note from Đỏ, Mây's younger brother, with whom Mây shared a special bond. Of course Đỏ expressed his feelings in his own words, but they might translate something like this: "Hang in there man. Don't be discouraged, we're all pulling for you and we know you'll come through. We're thinking of you all the time and send you our love and prayers. Thanks for being my big brother. Your Đỏ." Tears came to Mây's eyes as he thought of the little boy who had shown such loyalty and spunk in coming to the defense of his mother, so they could get into the seminary to see Mây on that day so many years ago in Cái Răng.

Fortified and reassured by the news from home and with the constant encouragement of Father Guy, Mây embarked upon his new activities with spirit. He breathed in the autumn air of this great free city as he walked through the tree-lined streets and nearby parks, their colours now changing to flaming red and yellow. He explored Montreal, joining the bustling crowds of subway passengers, workers and businessmen alike, as the Métro whisked him from station to station. From

Chinatown to Park Extension to the Marché Jean-Talon, immigrants such as himself were carving out a new existence in this land, and the accents of their languages mingled with those of the native Québécois and Anglo-Saxons. Mây walked through the underground passages of the Centre-Ville, lined with their chic boutiques, into the cavernous Gare Centrale, where commuters awaited the departure of their suburban trains with little fear of police identity checks or arbitrary arrest. And as Mây stopped a moment before the Cathedral which stands beside the station, no one questioned him suspiciously about his religious faith or his possible involvement with the Church.

Mây applied himself studiously to his French courses at one of the COFI (*Centre d'orientation et de formation des immigrants*) located only minutes away from his residence on Claremont Street. Again it was Father Guy who had arranged for his admission and ensured that he was placed at the right level. Some of the beginners remained without a clue for the whole term as their teachers strove valiantly to improve their communication skills, but Mây made steady progress in his group of about eight more advanced students. Father Guy also knew the importance of the "home stay" in language learning, so he invited Mây to come along with him to visit the Gauthier family in Saint-Jérôme, with whom Mây developed a lasting friendship. The Gauthiers were taken with feelings of sympathy and care for this earnest new arrival from a foreign country, and they were to prove much later on that they had not forgotten their Vietnamese friend.

Winter approached and temperatures skidded to unbelievable lows. Mây had never known anything like it, and, as Christmas approached, he spent the days shivering and sniffling in his room. Then one morning Father Guy appeared, surrounded by an air of secrecy. *"Va chercher ton manteau, nous allons à Ottawa!"* Why were they going to Ottawa? Mây wondered, but as no further explanations were forthcoming, he simply grabbed his tuque, coat, gloves and boots and followed Father Guy out the door and into the battered old Honda Civic sputtering at the curb. All was revealed as they headed out on highway 417 into Ontario in the direction of the capital city. As the snow-laden fields of the Canadian countryside slid by on either side, Father Guy explained that he had been planning a trip to his native Belgium, combined with a pilgrimage to some of the great sites associated with the Catholic heritage. When the time had come to purchase the ticket, Father Guy thought of Mây enduring the Canadian winter and still given to bouts of brooding over the horrors he had experienced in his flight from Việt Nam. On the spur of the moment, he had purchased two tickets instead of one. Now they were going to Ottawa to procure a "Certificate of Identity" and an authorization to travel abroad for Mây, who, although classified as a "landed immigrant", still did not have a Canadian passport. The document that Mây received was almost identical to a passport, except for its brown cover and the strict limitations concerning destinations and length of validity contained within. When provided with all the necessary visas, it conferred on Mây an official proof of his existence as a Canadian and his liberty to travel abroad, something he had never before had in his possession. In the whirl of excitement, Mây could barely comprehend that he was about to find himself in Rome, Lourdes, Paris and all those fabled places the French missionaries in Việt Nam had evoked so fondly. Yet it was true, and this moment in Mây's life passed like a dream of some other world, so that when it was over, Mây could hardly believe it had really taken place.

So it was that one morning towards the end of February, Mây and Father Guy boarded an Air France flight to Paris and thence directly to Rome. On their arrival in the Eternal City, they found lodging in a *pensione* adjacent to the Vatican. They spent several days admiring the ancient monuments of the City of Seven Hills and visiting the sacred places of the Vatican, the world's smallest independent state. They stood on Saint Peter's square and gazed up at the magnificent basilica bearing the name of the Founder of the Church, of whom Phêrô Hồ Văn Mây was one of the countless namesakes. They were received by the personal secretary of Pope John Paul II, Father Stanislaw Dziwisz, who was later elevated to the status of Archbishop of Krakow (Poland) and, most recently, Cardinal[7]. Although the Pope was occupied in a meeting with the cardinals, Father Dziwisz conveyed his greetings to the visitors and inquired at length about their individual itineraries. Along with

---

[7] March 24, 2006

millions of Catholics the world over, they prayed that Divine guidance might inspire the Holy Father and the leaders of the Church.

After five days in Rome, Mây and his sponsor were off to the shrine at Lourdes, in southern France, traveling through the sun-basked Italian countryside and along the French Riviera in the Renault 4L Father Guy had rented for the trip. At Lourdes, they joined the more than one million pilgrims who each year visit this site of the mystical experiences of Bernadette Soubiroux, a young farm girl reputed to have been visited by the Blessed Virgin on several occasions. Lourdes has also witnessed thousands of unexplained, but carefully documented recoveries from various afflictions among the faithful, which the Church has attributed to Divine intervention.

From Lourdes, Mây and Father Guy struck a beeline northeast to the village of Ars-sur-Formans in Burgundy. This was the home parish of Father Jean-Marie Vianney, the renowned Curé d'Ars, patron of all Catholic parish priests. In the chapel where the Curé's body lay exposed, Father Guy was privileged to say Mass for a small group of pilgrims. On leaving this site, Mây and Father Guy headed on to Dijon, where they visited another place of significance to Mây: the mother house of the Soeurs de la Providence, those French nuns who had provided Mây with his first schooling and their Vietnamese counterparts who had given him shelter before his escape. Then Guy and Mây were on the road again, going toward Belgium, the native land of Mây's sponsor. They entered Luxembourg and thirty minutes later exited this miniature country on their way to Brussels, the Belgian capital. From there, they went on to Louvain, site of the famous Université Catholique. Then they finally made their way to the city of Liège, Guy's birthplace, where they stayed for a few days with the family of Guy's brother, an engineer by profession. The brother, his wife and their children welcomed Mây into their home and showed him great hospitality during the time the two travelers spent with them.

Their European visit and pilgrimage nearing its end, Mây and Father Guy headed back to Paris, where they would be taking the plane to Montreal. Before leaving Paris, however, they visited yet another site, one that had special meaning for Mây: Rue du Bac and the quarters of the Société des Missions Étrangères. It was from here that, from the 17th century on, a total of more than 4,500 priests and seminarians, inspired by the examples of Alexandre de Rhodes, Pierre Lambert de la Motte and other pioneers, had left to fulfill their mission of Christianization in various Asian countries, notably Indochina. In return the Société provided food and lodging for many Asiatic students who came to Paris to complete their training. Mây was welcomed most warmly and introduced to several of his compatriots currently studying in Paris.

Adjacent to the seat of the Société des Missions Étrangères, the Chapelle Notre-Dame de la Médaille Miraculeuse commemorates the faith of Sister Catherine Labouré, a novice in the Convent who was inspired to propagate the particular design of a medal in honour of the Blessed Virgin, of which millions of specimens have since been stamped and distributed throughout the world as symbols of adherence to Christian faith and ideals and their truly miraculous effect on human lives. How many faithful hands in every country had touched these images, seeking solace and strength in the face of doubt and discouragement? Mây purchased one of the medals and carefully tucked it away in his vest pocket.

Once again Mây and Father Guy were at Charles de Gaulle Airport waiting for the departure of their return flight to Montréal. Once again Mây heard the loud-speaker crackle into life, as he had the first time in this very place only months before: *"... le vol... à destination de Montréal... passagers... à bord de l'appareil."* As Mây and Father Guy rose from their seats and headed up the gangway to the waiting plane, Mây realized this marvelous trip would soon be behind him. And, as enriching and inspirational as it had all been, Mây knew that his future now lay in that temporarily frozen land to which he was returning. High above the Atlantic, Mây had a long talk with Father Guy. Realistically, what did Father Guy think of Mây's chances of serving a useful life in Canada, a country so different and so far removed from his cherished homeland. And his lifelong goal of becoming a priest seemed as unattainable as ever. When would he ever attain ordination, the marker that had always receded before his eyes, as does the horizon before the advancing traveler. When? *"Peut-être pas tout de suite, mais plus tôt que tu ne le penses,"* replied Father Guy. Maybe not right away, but sooner than Mây might think. Father Guy reminded him that he, Hồ Văn Mây, had already passed many markers in his journey through life. Ordination, when it came, would only be one of them, and others would follow. And then, for the first time, Guy spoke in some detail of the idea he had in mind for Mây's future. The Church in Victoria, where Guy had been posted before coming to Montreal, was in dire need of new and committed clergy to serve in its many Catholic parishes. Father Guy was convinced that the Bishop of Victoria would evaluate Mây's previous studies and experiences favorably and make arrangements for him to complete the requirements for ordination within a reasonable period of time. Mây's enthusiasm quickened. Where was this Victoria? As soon as they got back, could they drive over and have a look? Father Guy stifled a chuckle. Hardly, he said, unless Mây was prepared to undertake a week-long 4,000 mile road trip. Victoria was on the other side of the continent, on the shores of the Pacific Ocean, that same ocean that also bathed, in its far reaches, the coast of Việt Nam.

As Mây settled back into his usual routine, the biting winds of winter gradually subsided and the first harbingers of spring began to appear. And now Father Guy came up with a new challenge for his Vietnamese friend. Mây should know, he confided, that when he got to Victoria, he would certainly need to have a car to get around to see his parishioners and perform all the services a member of the clergy is called upon to carry out. Distances were great, he pointed out, and time was often of the essence. The automobile was simply a fact of life, and Mây might as well learn to use it. Whereupon, he gave Mây $250 and directed him to the nearest reputable Auto-École. After an attentive perusal of the *Code de la route*, Mây passed the theoretical test with flying colours, scoring a thoroughly honorable 86. The actual driving part was a bit more difficult, given the heavy flow of traffic in the streets of Montreal; nevertheless, after much patient practice, Mây mastered this as well and was soon in possession of a valid *permis de conduire*, the driver's license which, more than a passport, certifies that each North American really does exist.

Father Guy's plans for Mây's future began to take concrete form. The Sacred Heart Parish, where Father Guy had previously served, had been contacted, and Father Harold Heard, the Parish Priest had indicated that he would be happy to introduce Mây to the Bishop with the recommendation that he be received into the Diocese. The Parish could offer some limited assistance while Mây was preparing to complete the requirements for the diaconate and ordination. Father Heard suggested that the most opportune moment for Mây's arrival in Victoria would be October, 1982, several months hence.

Mây's last summer in Montréal seemed to go on forever. Mây's thoughts were entirely directed toward his new destination and his future life as it seemed to be taking shape. Having finally located Victoria on the map and seen that the city was situated on an island, curiously called Vancouver Island and not to be confused with the city of Vancouver, which was elsewhere, Mây was curious to know what this place and its people were really like. Mây suspected it would be quite different from the islands he had previously known, Cù Lao Giêng and Cù Lao Tây, or even the island of Montreal, for it was not within a river, but lay off the coast entirely separated from the mainland by a wide stretch of water. And the people? Father Guy assured Mây that, although Catholics were in the minority, they were in general very supportive of the Church. They were in every important way like people the world over, each with his own faults and qualities, each with his own special needs.

Guy and Mây took one last excursion that summer. Mây had expressed the desire to set foot on the soil of the United States, that country which had generously received so many of his compatriots. So one day in July, after Mây had obtained a visa from the American consulate, they made the short drive down to the border, crossed the line at Alburg, Vermont, and continued down to Burlington and the surrounding area. The sparce but hardy population of the New England countryside had known only peace for nearly two hundred years and seemed quite oblivious to the problems of the rest of the world, yet many of their sons had served during the war in Việt Nam and shared the bitterness and humiliation of the conflict's final outcome. After this brief, largely symbolic visit, Mây and Father Guy headed back to Montréal, where Mây was to make his final preparations for departure, and crossing the continent to Victoria. The Fathers of the Fraternité Sacerdotale were disappointed that Mây had decided not to remain among them, but

Mây's decision had been made. It was not without some regrets, however, for he would be leaving many friends, chief among whom was his sponsor, Father Guy.

Father Guy drove Mây to Dorval Airport that day in October. As Mây passed through the checking area into the waiting room, he looked back and caught a last glimpse of his friend standing behind the roped-off area. Mây could not help but think that God had chosen Father Guy Merveille for a special mission in this world. Here was a man who, like the Good Samaritan of the Bible, refused to "pass by on the other side." He had generously spent the better part of his salary, and even borrowed from friends, to help a neighbour in need. More than that, he had shown a genuine interest in the person he was helping, not just as a sponsor, but as a friend. He was a listener as well as a counselor and made the Other's hopes and aspirations his own. To sum it up, he was a Good Priest and a Good Man, and Mây wondered if he could ever repay the debt of gratitude he owed to Father Guy Merveille.

IX. Adaptation

A policeman was waiting to take Mây into custody as he stepped off the plane at Victoria Airport.

Have no fear, dear reader, the man who greeted Mây at the airport, Mr. Clifford Dalsin, although indeed a policeman by profession, was acting on behalf of Sacred Heart Parish. He belonged to a group of parishioners who had volunteered to show Mây their hospitality by taking him into their homes, acquainting him with family life and customs in this corner of the world and helping him to learn the language during his period of adaptation. Clifford and his wife Daphne, a nurse, would be the first to receive Mây, giving him room and board for a month, before Mây moved on to the next family. And so it would continue until the Diocese could give Mây an official appointment. In the meantime Mây would assist Father Heard in his duties at Sacred Heart Church. The Dalsins and their five adolescent children provided Mây with a good introduction to the busy life of a typical North American family and a demonstration of their friendship and concern for the newcomer in their community.

Father Heard lost no time in presenting Mây to Bishop Rémi de Roo. The Bishop welcomed Mây into the Diocese, but was rather vague concerning exactly how Mây might fulfill the requirements leading to the diaconate and the priesthood. "All in good time, all in good time," he said, patting Mây on the shoulder. Then the Bishop gave Father Heard to understand that during all this "good time", Mây's welfare was to remain in the hands of Sacred Heart Parish. The Bishop seemed preoccupied with other urgent problems facing the Church, and Mây wondered if he would even remember their meeting, much less take any immediate action to further Mây's progression toward the priesthood.

Sacred Heart Parish was soon to celebrate its fiftieth anniversary. Established as a mission in 1936 by Bishop John McDonald and initially administered by priests from the Cathedral, Sacred Heart was designated as a parish in 1941 by Bishop John C. Cody. The first church, constructed in 1936, was replaced by a spacious new building in 1966. Over the course of the years, many distinguished pastors had served the Parish, two of whom had shared Mây's experience as refugees. Father Jan Planetta, ordained in Poland before the Second World War, was arrested by the Gestapo in 1939 and interned in a concentration camp until 1945. The Parish sponsored his immigration to Canada and he became its pastor in 1956. Father Heard, the current pastor, had been studying at a seminary in France when that country was invaded by the German army in 1940 and had managed to escape to England the day before the fall of France.

Mây assumed a helpful, if somewhat limited role in the activities of Sacred Heart Parish. He assisted Father Heard in all the functions that a lay person, as Mây was still considered to be, might be permitted by the Church to perform. In addition to his presence as an altar server at regular Masses, his occupations included various organizational activities, participation in the catechism program and setting up and conducting prayer meetings for certain groups within the church. Among these latter was the group Mây organized for Vietnamese parishioners, several of whom had only recently arrived in Canada, having been sponsored by Father Guy during his tenure at Sacred Heart Parish.

In return for these services, Mây received a monthly stipend of $150 in addition to the room and board provided by his various hosts in the parish. It was a frugal existence, to say the least, and one that contrasted sharply with the seemingly opulent life-style of the general citizenry. Nevertheless, on a spiritual and cultural level, the compensations were great. Mây had been in this sort of situation many times before, as a devoted assistant to the titular priest in different parishes in Việt Nam, where he had shared the spiritual experiences of parishioners in their own particular cultural contexts. Mây remembered his Chinese friends in Hòn Chông and Rảy Mới, the hard-working population of Phước Hảo Parish, where Mây had done his pastoral service, and the brave and steadfast people of An Long, where Mây and Father Đệ had endured the persecution of the Việt Cộng.

Mây's host families represented a range of professions and a good cross section of Canadian life. In most cases, both husband and wife held jobs, raised children or helped raise grandchildren and were in addition active in the Church and in various charitable organizations. Two of the men were carpenters, several men and women were school teachers, one was a musician, others devoted themselves to a variety of occupations. Children in these families ranged from infants to young adults. Often elderly grandparents were also living in the homes. Mây could observe the interplay of age, interests and individual character in determining the fabric of family relationships within this culture, so different from his own.

One facet of these relationships surprised Mây greatly. Vietnamese culture and language mark hierarchy within the family according to age very precisely, as a sign of respect. An older brother or sister may call his younger siblings by their given names, but the younger ones replace the name with a more honorific term when speaking to their elders. Not only are special terms of address used when speaking to older people, the form used to designate oneself also varies according to the age of the other person. Imagine Mây's astonishment, then, when he heard a five-year-old refer to his elderly grandfather as "John": "Is John coming this afternoon?" Mây soon realized that no disrespect was intended. In our evolving culture, more emphasis is placed on the intimacy and equality of relationships than the advantages that accrue with age or position. Nevertheless, Mây was a bit saddened, as many are, by what might appear to be the loss of a sense of value for the efforts and contributions of those who go before us, as translated in the way we speak to them. Then again, Mây had only to think of that other five-year-old, waiting on the curb in front of Sacred Heart Church, who had suddenly perceived his grandfather getting out of a parked car and hobbling toward him. His face radiant with joy and excitement, oblivious to all around him, the boy called out in eager anticipation, "Nono! Nono!" As Mây put out his hand to hold him back from the moving cars, the boy looked up at Mây with an expression of such love and pride as rarely seen on the faces of adults. "But it's Nono! It's *my* Nono!" The bond between young and old is a universal thing, and one of God's great gifts to humanity.

As Mây went from family to family, his command of English began to improve and he became more aware of both the universality and the particularities of human experience. Real affection developed between the immigrant and his hosts, but inevitably the constant change of environment began to take its toll on Mây's morale. There was another nagging thought which contributed to his increasing despondency. He had been living in this land of plenty for almost two years, yet he hadn't been able to send a cent back to his family in Việt Nam. He knew that his father was struggling to pay back the debts incurred for his escape three years before; his father's honour would not permit him to do otherwise, even if it meant less food on the table all around. What could Mây do with just a hundred and fifty dollars a month? "Open a savings account at the bank and put a little money in each month," advised Mr. Vince Sullivan, Mây's current host, and added wisely, "Dollars out of little pennies grow!" Whereupon, he led Mây to the local branch of the Canadian Imperial Bank of Commerce, took fifty dollars out of his wallet and opened a savings account in Mây's name. Mây fingered his passbook in disbelief. Here he was, a man with money in the bank, a thing absolutely unheard of in his native village. Every month thereafter he took ten dollars out of his pittance and handed them over to a somewhat bemused bank teller for deposit in his account, but the "little pennies" seemed to experience growing pains, and his balance remained frustratingly small.

Mr. Sullivan was aware of Mây's plight, and a meeting with the other parishioners was arranged to see what could be done for their fledgling servant of the Church. It was decided that Mr. Sullivan should write a letter to the Bishop or the Vicar General, who had given no previous sign of interest in Mây's case. Taking pen in hand, this kind man, who would always remain Mây's friend and supporter, wrote a moving letter to the Bishop in which he stressed Mây's qualities and his devotion to the goal he had set for himself, that of becoming a priest. He also hinted at Mây's current feelings of disarray: "He is like a lost sheep who would be the shepherd." A few days later, Mr. Sullivan received a reply from the Vicar General thanking him for his input and stating that "a final decision will be reached in the near future." But the weeks dragged on and there was no further news from the Diocese. Mây regretfully said goodbye to the Sullivans, with whom he had remained more than two months, and moved on to his next hosts.

Several moves later, Mây found himself alone in a small, sparsely furnished room of which an elderly widower had given him the use. Mây was profoundly discouraged by the way things were going and troubled by new doubts about his future. Was he not now a man of forty, in full possession of certain skills and physical capacities, a man who could easily find employment on the labour market? A new government employment center, called "Manpower", had just opened in Victoria, and tales of fabulous opportunities were rife. Within months Mây could be earning a salary of unheard of proportions! But then, Oh God! What of the priesthood, the reason for his escape from his native land and the acceptance of all the dangers, sufferings and difficulties that went along with it? How could Mây even think of such a thing? And yet…

Overtaken by powerful feelings of temptation, Mây sought strength in prayer. He recited the rosary for several hours that evening before falling into a convulsive sleep, troubled by strange nightmares. Out of a churning sea of dark clouds the great Temple of Manpower rose, stone upon grey stone, until it reached the sky. Bright lights gleamed from within its lower, glass-encased reaches. Through the swinging doors of its gaping portals streamed a multitude of shadowy figures, as though drawn within by some mysterious force. Beside the massive Temple of Manpower, the delicate Shrine of Godpower flickered bravely for a moment, then dimmed and dissolved in the distance. Now a succession of familiar faces faded in and out over these images: Phạn and Ngự, Mây's brothers and sisters, Father Đệ, a bearded general, Catherine Labouré, the Curé d'Ars, Guy Merveille and Vince Sullivan, they were all there, their expressions reflecting no reproach, but rather an infinite sadness. Then the whole construction began to crumble, sucking in the swirl of faces, and came crashing down, its fragments engulfed by the sea of clouds.

Mây awoke with a start, sweating profusely. The air was filled with the sounds of a summer morning, but Mây was unaware of their beauty. Sleep had brought him no rest and his inner conflict had known no resolution. He sat on the edge of his cot, as if frozen in despair and indecision. Clearly, it was time for some intervention from On High.

Mr. Stephanex Chester, Mây's landlord, was rapping on the door. Would Mây please come into the living room and take a telephone call from someone who should know better than to call at this early hour. Mây hurriedly pulled on a pair of pants, followed Mr. Chester into the latter's private quarters and picked up the receiver. The voice coming through the wire identified itself as that of Father Sigismond Lajoie, Vicar General of the Diocese of Victoria. Mây was instructed to pack up his belongings and come down to the Chancery at once. A decision by the Bishop's Council had been reached in Mây's case.

The Vicar General was waiting impatiently for Mây when he arrived at the Chancery. "We have much to do," he said to Mây. "You're leaving for Ottawa in two days."

Mây was mystified and thought for a moment he was back in Montreal with Father Guy, about to set off for the nation's capital in search of some official proof of his existence. True, his Certificate of Identity had now expired, but was it really necessary to cross the continent to have it renewed? And did this mean he was being sent off to some other country?

"No, no," replied Father Lajoie to Mây's anxious inquiry. "Don't worry, you can have your Certificate renewed when you're there, if you like. But that's not the reason you're going to Ottawa. You'll be staying there for a while. The Bishop has arranged for your admission to Saint Paul University, where you will complete the requirements for your ordination as a priest. Now come along, we have to go to the Totem Travel Agency so you can get a ticket."

Mây could hardly believe his ears. So the Bishop hadn't forgotten him after all! Mây felt a flush of joy, quickly tempered by the sobering realization that his finances would not allow him to purchase air fare to Ottawa. This he regretfully explained to Father Lajoie. "Oh, really!" huffed the Vicar General, who was growing weary of Mây's incessant objections. "All right," he continued, "we'll take care of that, but I hope you at least have enough money to buy yourself some luggage and a decent set of clothes. No? Good Lord, man, what have you been doing with your salary?" Father Lajoie had apparently forgotten that for the last eight months Mây had been living on charitable donations. "Very well," he sighed, "I'll have five hundred dollars withdrawn from our account for your immediate expenses. Once you're in Ottawa, arrangements have been made for you to be taken in charge by the University, so, unless you intend to maintain a high-profile living style, you should be all right. Now is there anything further?"

No, there was nothing further, replied Mây, somewhat dazzled by the prospect of this sudden wealth. He was, however, considerably less wealthy when, after acquiring a suitcase, a winter parka, gloves and a new pair of boots, he boarded the Air Canada direct flight to Ottawa two days later.

Mây waited with a certain anxiety at the arrival gate in Ottawa Airport, showing his sign marked "Peter Ho, Victoria" to any and all likely-looking representatives of Saint Paul University. Finally a man approached, greeted Mây and introduced himself as a person "connected" with the University. Connected? The individual in question was the University's Rector, Father Gilles Cazabon![8] Now it might seem unusual for a University that a new student should be personally welcomed by the Rector, but then Saint Paul University was that kind of institution! Founded in 1848 by Bishop Joseph-Eugène Guigues, the College of Bytown, later renamed College of Ottawa, received official recognition as a university in 1866 and a pontifical charter in 1889. In 1933, the institution for-

---

[8] Later Bishop of the Diocese of Saint-Jérôme, Québec

mally acquired the French designation "Université d'Ottawa" and began a steady expansion through the succeeding decades until it included nine faculties, covering all academic areas, as well as four specialized schools. The University occupied a large tract of land in the heart of Ottawa and had become an important part of the life of Canada's capital city. In 1965, it was decided that the University's secular and religious orientations should be more clearly defined. The University of Ottawa became an independent, though associated institution, secular in nature, whereas the newly-designated Saint Paul University retained its educational functions within a Christian tradition and notably, in its Faculty of Theology, that of the formation of future deacons and priests in the Catholic Church.

It was in this more personal environment that Mây undertook a one-year program designed to complete the studies that had been interrupted eight years previously at Saint-Sulpice Seminary in Vĩnh Long. He was given a program of eleven subject matters, ranging from ethics to Church dogma, to be sanctioned by final examinations at the end of the year. For Mây, it was mostly a review of his training at Vĩnh Long; nevertheless, it was a necessary one, for so much time, filled with so many trials, had passed since then.

However, there were many links with the past. Although the University was very definitely a Catholic institution, it also sought to acquaint its students with other theological traditions, thus promoting a greater degree of ecumenism. Mây fondly remembered Father Tran Thai Dinh and his instruction of Buddhist philosophy at the very Catholic Saint-Sulpice Seminary in Vĩnh Long!

The year Mây had spent in Victoria had been quite different from the one in Montreal. Now Mây was back in an environment which recalled his previous experience. There was of course the close association with his fellow students, which brought to mind Mây's fellowship with the Fathers of the Fraternité Sacerdotale. And the French-English bilingualism, which was one of the cornerstones of Saint Paul University, contrasted sharply with the almost exclusively English atmosphere of Victoria. Courses at Saint Paul were given indifferently in French or English, and all of the teachers and most of the students were fluent in both languages.

Then, as a less agreeable aspect of the difference, there was the climate! The slightest chill in the air in Victoria had been interpreted by the natives as a frightful cold wave, but here in Ottawa, as winter set in, temperatures dipped to levels even lower than those of Montreal, and the biting winds turned every step out of doors into a major exploit of climatic endurance. Such excursions were a necessary fact of life, for residences, refectories, classrooms and libraries were not all in the same location. Very recently [9], the University has acquired a new integrated facility, and on the occasion of

---

[9] December 2005

its inauguration, the current rector remarked: "Students in our residence will find it much easier and more inviting to head over to the University Library for reading and consultation now than when they had to decide whether it was a good idea to head out into minus thirty degree weather on a cold January night to do a little extra reading on a topic of particular interest to them." Which was what Mây had to do, and he wished he'd spent a few more of his five hundred dollars, of which very little now remained, on some truly Arctic apparel.

Mây made many acquaintances among the students and teachers at Saint Paul. In particular, he became good friends with Father Peter Surin, a priest from Thailand who was doing graduate work in Canada before returning to take up a teaching position in his native country. The two homonyms, Peter Hồ and Peter Surin, spent many hours together reviewing their course work and reflecting on the cultural differences between North America and their own part of the world. When Mây was crossing Cambodia during his escape, he had seen Thailand as a foreign land, so distant it appeared almost unattainable. Now, as he chatted with his friend, their two countries were as one. Although historically Thailand and Việt Nam have often been at odds, they were united in this friendship, particularly so since the two men shared the same religious calling. Surin is a common name in Thailand, even designating a city and province not far removed from the camp where Mây had spent such terrible hours. The warm, empathetic camaraderie demonstrated by Peter Surin, as well as his deep spiritual commitment, erased from Mây's mind the memory of those wild Thai soldiers at NW9. Beyond this particular example, Mây realized that good and evil exist side by side in all parts of the world and in all realms of society. Remembering the meaning of the word "catholic" as "universal", Mây reflected that the role of the Church should be to everywhere promote the good and diminish the evil on both a personal and a societal level: in other words, to work toward the brotherhood of all men and women, sons and daughters of the same Father, following the teachings of the Lord Jesus Christ. As the priest who Mây hoped soon to become, this would be Mây's own personal commitment, whatever he might be doing and wherever he might be.

X. Milestones

One day in March, 1984, as Mây and Peter Surin were relaxing outside the doors of the Saint Paul dining hall, awaiting the call to partake of terrestrial nourishment, Mây was informed that he had a telephone call from the Bishop of Victoria. The Bishop wanted to know how things were going for Mây at the University. Very well indeed, Mây replied, he had completed the course work and was now enjoying a short break before the final examinations. Could Mây spare him three days, inquired the Bishop. A special retreat had been planned at the Victoria Diocese and on this occasion it was intended to hold a ceremony in which Mây would be introduced into the diaconate of the Church. So could Mây please book a return ticket to Victoria, at the Diocese's expense, of course. He would be back in Ottawa in time for the final examinations. Mây replied that he would certainly obey these instructions, thanked the Bishop, set down the receiver and stood there a moment in total astonishment. A deacon in the Church! His first official admission to the clergy! Could ordination be far behind?

Mây forgot about lunch, and after telling Father Surin the good news, went off to pack his bag and make his reservation. In reality, he knew full well what admission to the diaconate signified. In the hierarchy of Holy Orders of the Catholic Church, the diaconate is received prior to priesthood, and is a necessary step toward ordination, which normally follows fairly soon thereafter.

The deacon has, however, his own special functions within the Church, including the proclamation of the gospel, preaching to the faithful, administering baptism and the right to give communion. Sometimes a deacon is temporarily in charge of a parish during the absence of the resident priest. Needless to say, accession to the diaconate is a very important event in the life of a man of the Church, and is always marked by a solemn and significant ceremony.

Once again, Mây was winging his way toward Victoria. Without exactly being a member of the "Jet Set", he was nevertheless becoming a seasoned air traveler. The ceremony of introduction to the diaconate took place shortly after Mây's arrival. It was held in the chapel of Queenswood House at the Convent of the Sisters of Saint Ann on March 30, 1984. The cinderblock chapel is nestled between tall pines and red-barked arbutus trees on the outskirts of Victoria. In a way, the setting has something about it which might call Mây's homeland to mind. The air is different of course, as are the architecture and the surrounding vegetation. But the integration of a construction of human hands in a purely natural environment is not unlike that of the churches of Việt Nam. For Mây, on that day, it was a sacred place of serenity and fulfillment. It was not a Basilica or a Cathedral or even the historic downtown chapel of Saint Ann's Academy, which had fallen into disrepair and was home to squatters. It was, however, a milestone on Mây's life journey, and one that he would long remember. The ceremony and Holy Mass were presided over by Archbishop Emmette Carter and Bishop Remi de Roo, with Father Heard and other priests and deacons of the Victoria area in attendance. Mây was received into the diaconate along with Michael Lapierre, who was later to become Chancellor and Vicar General of the Victoria Diocese. Such was not Mây's ambition, for it was as a parish priest that he felt he could best serve the Church and ordination was no longer a faint and distant goal, but rather an imminent reality. In the meantime, Mây resolved to fulfil his duties as a deacon to the very best of his ability in order to merit the Bishop's confidence and all the assistance the Diocese had afforded him.

Let us leave Deacon Hồ to pursue his career of "frequent flyer", much to the delight of the Totem Travel Agency, as he flies back to Ottawa for final examinations and then returns to Victoria to assume his duties as deacon. We shall meet him again, as he undertakes another journey, by land this time, to Port Hardy, a community on the northernmost tip of Vancouver Island.

Our new deacon was being sent to Port Hardy to replace the current parish priest, an American, Father Tranor, who was returning to the United States. For two months, Deacon Hồ would be in charge of the parish until a permanent replacement could be appointed.

Port Hardy, named for a British vice-admiral, is aptly designated in a more general sense, for its fewer than five thousand inhabitants are a hardy people. Most are en-gaged in three resource-based industries, logging, fishing and mining, although tourism has become an important source of revenue in recent years. At the time of Deacon Hồ's visit, the nearby Island Copper Mine furnished the bulk of employment. In spite of the recent completion of Highway 19, linking the town to the southern communities, and the inauguration of a ferry service to Prince Rupert on the coast, Port Hardy lived in relative isolation from the rest of the world, an isolation which greatly increased as night fell and the community, devoid of street lighting, sank into the total darkness of the surrounding wilderness. For Mây, raised in the heavily populated Mekong Delta and familiar only with urban areas of Canada, it was a strange and somewhat frightening environment. His days, however, were completely occupied by the many activities of the parish for which he alone was responsible. The experience was not new to Mây, who had lived the same situation at Rẫy Mới after Father Lượng's departure and at An Long after the arrest of Father Đệ. Communion services were held, the hosts having been previously consecrated by the now departed priest. There were baptisms and funeral services, visits to the school and hospital, and many other contacts with the local population. The time passed quickly for Deacon Hồ until, just as he was beginning to develop a real bond with these people, he was informed that the new permanent priest, Father Richard Caldwell, was arriving to take over his duties. Mây was to return to Victoria, where important events were soon to take place.

A long while ago, on a rice farm in southern Indochina, a little boy sat watching his father's cattle swish their tails back and forth against a lush green background of vegetation, beyond which a great river flowed gently to the horizon. The sky above seemed to stretch infinitely upwards in a great expanse of towering cloud formations. Where did it go, that sky, the boy wondered? And what if you were up there on one of those clouds, looking down? What would you see? You'd see a boy sitting on a piece of wood and some cattle swishing their tails, but really they'd just be tiny spots in the middle of a big green field. Would it matter to someone up there what the spots did, how they moved around, where they went? The boy's mother and father said it did very much matter, and that's why they worked so hard all day and weren't just bandits taking things away from other people. That was why they loved their children and cared about what the boy and his brothers and sisters were doing. That was why they went to Mass, where the priest helped them to pray to Lord God to be good and to be good to others. Then, thinking of the priest, the boy held up one of the mud biscuits he had been forming with his fingers and recited the words he had heard that morning at Mass: "*Đây là Chiên Thiên Chúa...* This is the lamb of God who takes away the sins of the world. Happy are those who are called to his supper." The boy knew you didn't always stay the way you are. No, you grew up and went and did things in the world. His mother and father kept saying they wanted him to grow up and be a priest. Well, that's what he wanted too, and that's what he would do! The little boy stood up and began to prod the cattle back towards their stall, back to the thatch-walled buildings where his mother and father, his brothers and sisters, his friends and enemies and thousands of others were waiting for him, waiting to walk along with him a part of the way.

Many years and a million miles later, the boy stood before the altar of a great Cathedral in a foreign city. A bishop was clothing him in a white robe. The boy, who was now a man, was about to be ordained as a priest in the Catholic Church.

Since his return from Port Hardy, Mây had been staying with the Sullivans and assisting Father Lajoie, who had assumed the responsibility of Sacred Heart Parish after the departure of Father Heard. While he was performing these duties, Mây had received the news of his impending ordination and even the date on which this was to take place: December 8th, 1984. The ceremony would be held at Saint Andrew's Cathedral in downtown Victoria with Bishop Remi de Roo once again presiding. Mây had time to flash off the news to friends and acquaintances far and wide. Taking advantage of the winter break at Saint Paul University, Father Surin promised to be in attendance. And then, oh joy! Father Guy Merveille would also come and give the homily on this occasion! Just days before the ceremony, Mây was surprised to see the FedEx man at the door with a large package for a Deacon Peter Hồ, coming from Saint-Jérôme, Quebec. The Gauthier family had not forgotten their Vietnamese friend, and, along with their card of congratulations, had sent a handsome television set, so that the new priest might keep abreast of what was going on in the world! Of course, all of the families who had helped Mây through his period of adaptation in Victoria were invited, as well as his many friends in the Vietnamese community. It promised to be quite an occasion!

In a quiet moment, Mây addressed an envelope to Anh Hồ Văn Ngự, Tân Hòa, Đồng Tháp, Việt Nam. In his letter, which he knew would only arrive weeks later, Mây lovingly informed his father that Phạn's dream had finally come to realization and that, thanks to all of their help, in a few days he would be ordained as a priest.

December 8th came, Hồ Văn Mây entered the Cathedral as a deacon, and, after a beautiful and reverential ceremony, emerged as Father Peter Hồ, priest. The following day, Father Peter celebrated his own first Mass at Sacred Heart Church. On this occasion as well, Father Guy delivered the homily. He once again stressed the fact that "catholic" means "universal" and that the Church receives a gift from God when, as a priest, a person from another country and another culture brings his talent, his knowledge and his understanding to the people he is serving. After the Mass, the Fathers Guy, Peter Hồ and Peter Surin exchanged goodbyes, but they all promised to keep in close contact, and in fact, both Father Guy Merveille and Father Peter Surin were to touch Father

Peter Hồ's life again, either shortly thereafter or in many years to come.

Another celebration, this one strictly private, was held somewhat later in Tân Hòa. Some thirty members of the extended family of Hồ Văn Ngự, united around a well garnished table, had gathered together, unbeknownst to the local authorities who were ill-disposed to sanctioning such assemblies. A camera and some black and white film had been found to capture the event for posterity. In the middle of the meal, the click of a spoon on a bowl announced a solemn interruption of the festivities. A large banner was raised for everyone to see and was greeted with prolonged applause all around. Written in tall, neat letters were the words: *Chúc Mừng Tân Linh Mục* "Congratulations to the Newly Ordained Priest", followed by the date, February 9, 1985.

XI. The Road Beyond

Father Hồ's first assignment was to assume duties as associate pastor at Sacred Heart Parish, an expansion of his previous activities there. After six months, he was transferred to Saint Andrew's Cathedral and Parish, where he was to remain almost nine years. The Cathedral, which replaced a structure dating from 1858, was opened in 1892, the initial Mass being celebrated by Bishop J.N. Lemmens. The Cathedral is an imposing edifice inspired by the architecture of similar churches in Quebec and renowned for its magnificent stained-glass windows. At the time of Mây's appointment, the principal pastor of the parish was Monsignor Philip Hanley, until he was called to another Victoria parish, Saint Patrick's, and was replaced by Father Terry McNamara. Saint Andrew's is the largest parish in the Victoria Diocese, serving a significant indigenous community as well as countless Catholic visitors from Canada, the United States and other countries. One of the most important activities of the parish is the maintenance of an elementary school which, in conjunction with the high school operated by the Diocese, allows for a full education inspired by Christian values up to that level. Father Peter Hồ, that is to say Phê-rô Hồ Văn Mây, was charged with all the usual responsibilities of a priest at the Cathedral and, in addition, the functions of chaplain in the elementary school.

What's in a name?

Here we come to an important decision, one that concerns an essential question of identity. Now that he is a priest, shall we continue to refer to our protagonist by his given name, Mây, or shall we call him Father Peter, or would the more distant Father Hồ be appropriate? Certainly, the new passport which was issued after the man in question became a Canadian citizen identifies the bearer as Peter Ho (with no accents), and is signed as such. Gone are the couple of loops ending in a very legible "May" (with no accent) which adorned the Certificate of Identity in 1981. And of course the new priest would soon be known to the majority of his parishioners as Father Peter or Father Ho. But what of that boy in the field watching the cattle? Who was he? And our subject might now well ask himself, "Who am I?"

Now in a certain sense it is true that in becoming a priest one becomes a new, or better said, a renewed person. Did not the apostle Paul say to the Colossians:

> *...ye have put off the old man with his deeds; And have put on the new man, which is renewed in knowledge after the image of him that created him...* (Col.3: 9-10).

And Paul himself was never referred to as Saul after his experience on the road to Damascus. These were however conversions, the whole life of the persons concerned being in contradiction with their previous existences. In Mây's case, it is the opinion of the author, it was a matter of confirmation rather than conversion, for from his earliest memories, despite periods of wrenching doubt and uncertainty, he was sustained by an ever growing and ultimately unshakeable faith in his religion and in his calling. This faith was inspired and nurtured by loving parents, who, being at the top of the Vietnamese family structure, had the right to call *all* of their children by their first (last) names. So there is also the consideration of respect for one's origins that must be weighed in the balance in the choice of a name. Further, the man who becomes a priest also remains a man, and the sum of that man's previous experiences is an essential part of his new existence. The priest may be God's emissary, God's translator, God's man-on-the-spot, as it were; he does not become God himself. Neither does he become some minor deity enthroned on a hill awaiting homage from his obedient subjects. No, he is intimately involved in the life of the people he serves as well as in the evolution of his own personal relation to the Deity. These are ongoing commitments, renewed and confirmed by ordination, but in reality the continuation of a life inspired by the same ideals. After much soul-searching, the author of this brief account of one man's life has decided, perhaps somewhat arbitrarily, to continue to call his subject by any name that he pleases, trusting the reader will understand to whom he is referring.

And now, just what is a priest and what does a priest do? Mây quickly came to realize the truth of the words Father Guy had spoken to him when they were coming back on the plane from Europe. Ordination was not the end of the road, but simply a milestone on the way, the beginning of a new leg on Mây's journey. It was to be a journey of discovery: discovery of the joys, the cares, the responsibilities, the humility of the priesthood.

First of all, the priest is a busy man; Mây knew that already. People who imagine the priest to be quietly passing his time in a comfortable armchair, meditating the content of a ten-minute sermon for the coming Sunday, have no idea of the number of services he is called upon to perform: daily Mass, vigils, confessions, hospital visits, wedding arrangements, funerals, the consolation of bereaved parishioners, baptisms, catechism lessons, parish council meetings, the list goes on. And the priest does also live in our everyday world, with many of the usual cares and troubles everyone faces: financial worries, travel expenses, the problem of keeping a twenty-year old car on the road. Yet the priest must be able to find ample time for study, contemplation and prayer. Without this essential aspect, as a Swiss pastor recently put it[10], the "puzzle of life" lacks that last important piece, without which the rest doesn't make any sense.

Mây discovered that the life of a priest can be lonely at times. Lacking the companionship of a physical

---

[10] Martin Fontana, "Il puzzle dalla veta", *La Quotidiana*, May 12, 2006.

partner, the priest must face all those little hurts of life, the incomprehension and sometimes the outright hostility of those around him, swallow his pride and keep his feelings to himself. People are not always happy with their priest. They would like him to change one of the Ten Commandments on their behalf or make an exception to Church doctrine this one time, saying "We won't mention this to the Pope." The priest cannot agree, as much as he might like to have such an easy solution at hand. But neither can he shed his responsibility to assist people in finding help through their faith in order to face these difficult problems or situations.

And yet, as his years of service unfolded at Saint Andrew's and beyond, Father Hồ would not have had his life any other way, for he also knew the joys of priest-hood: the joy of sharing a penitent's happiness on receiving absolution, the joy of helping parishioners with a few words of encouragement, admiration, consolation or advice, the supreme joy, ever renewed, of sharing in the divine mysteries of the Mass and Holy Communion.

Another one of these joys was Father Peter's weekly visits to Saint Andrew's School. There were many children of different origins in the catechism classes, including several sons and daughters of the Vietnamese refugees Father Guy had sponsored. Father Peter thanked God that the lives of these children had been spared and that they could grow in the faith of their parents in a climate of freedom. Father Peter's quiet good humour and his somewhat unusual verbalizations endeared him to the English-speaking students. As for those with a French background, one can imagine their astonishment on hearing Father Peter suddenly break into a stirring rendition of a Belgian Boy Scout[11] marching song, which no doubt came to him by way of Father Guy:

> *Le coq est mort!*
> *Le coq est mort!*
>
> *Il ne fera plus*
> *Cocodi, cocoda!*

Despite these occasional moments of levity, Mây approached his instruction with earnestness and sincerity, for he knew how important his own father's insistence on regular religious practice had been in his upbringing. Mây remembered too the "Good Pastors" of Việt Nam whom he had served as a child. Men of truth, faith and prayer, they had played no little role in fostering his budding vocation. Mây's secret hope was that, among these boys and girls now assembled before him, some one or ones might follow in his footsteps and join the ranks of servants of Christ and of the Church.

With the approach of summer, Mây began to consider the possibility of a short visit to Montreal to recharge his spiritual batteries in contact with Guy Merveille and the

---

[11] In French-speaking Europe, the Scouting movement is conducted in two parallel organizations: *Les Scouts* (Catholic) and *Les Éclaireurs* (Protestant).

Fathers of the Fraternité Sacerdotale. As the month of July offered some respite from Mây's usual duties, he made another visit to Totem Travel, and was soon once again winging his way to the East. In Montreal, he was met by Guy and Father Hàm, and the three friends immediately repaired to an excellent Vietnamese restaurant on Lacombe Street in the Côte-des-Neiges district, where they shared their experiences of the past few years over steaming bowls of *phở* (beef noodle soup) and plates of *bánh xèo* (stuffed crepes). Mây told Father Guy that one of his ambitions was to follow Guy's example and become a sponsor for Vietnamese and other refugees seeking a way to leave their detention camps in various Southeast Asian countries and come to Canada. *"Une excellente idée!"* exclaimed Father Guy, and he encouraged Mây to put the plan into action as soon as it would be financially possible for him to do so.

During his stay in Montreal, Mây said his first Mass in French at the house of the Fraternité Sacerdotale, and a second in the chapel of Louis-Hippolyte Lafontaine Hospital, before a simple altar and crucifix, with patients and employees of the hospital in attendance. This was an especially moving experience, for it was here that Father Guy performed his regular services as Chaplain of the institution, and it symbolized the devotion of men of the Church to the service of people of all conditions, in whatever particular situation they may find themselves.

This was the last time Mây would see Father Guy. After Mây's return to Victoria, taken up by their respective cares and occupations, they gradually fell out of touch. A few years later Mây heard that Father Guy had died, although he was unable to learn exactly when and in what circumstances.

Mây knew how urgent the problem of refugee sponsorship was; however, his own financial situation suffered a blow which caused the plan to be momentarily put on hold. Father Hồ's desire to be of assistance to parishioners in need had led him to become a guarantor for certain business arrangements, which, although certainly worthy acts of Christian charity, turned out to be financially disastrous for the good priest. Since he had already committed a good portion of his salary to the repayment of the debts his father had incurred for Mây's escape from Việt Nam, when one added in the new obligations, there was precious little left for other purposes. However, a new plan to pursue the aims Mây had vowed to accomplish was not long in taking shape.

Through Monsignor Philip Hanley, Father Peter had become acquainted with Hanley's brother-in-law, Karel Van Bourgondien. A Dutchman who had lived in the former Netherlands East Indies, Van Bourgondien was well aware of the refugee problem. In addition, he was in the wholesale grocery trade and possessed a keen sense of business acumen. When Father Peter explained his desires to him, Van Bourgondien suggested that he and his wife Eleanor might join Father Peter in forming a charitable foundation to be known as the Ho Mission Refugee Association. The Association, which was formally organized in 1987, would apply for status as a recognized charity, contributions to the fund being therefore deductible from the income tax of the contributor. This was a necessary condition for any type of serious charitable fundraising. An independent auditor was appointed to oversee the financial dealings of the Association, and an active campaign to solicit contributions from Catholic parishioners was undertaken.

Contributors proved to be very generous, and it was soon possible to begin sponsoring refugees. Many of these brave people had passed through trials that paralleled Mây's own experiences. One man had spent more than four years in a detention camp in Malaysia, separated from his wife and children, until the Ho Missions permitted them all to be reunited in Canada. Another had seen fourteen members of his party perish at sea and survived himself only by the sheerest of chances. Some of the refugees were from Mây's home area. One of Mây's nephews, Hồ Văn Tuyền, the son of his elder brother Toà and a mere boy of twelve at the time of Mây's ordination, was able to join his uncle in Victoria, where he later married and is now beginning his own family.

Among the refugees sponsored by Ho Missions was a former soldier who had been one of those who accompanied the officer that arrested Hồ Văn Ngự after Mây's escape. When the man realized just who his sponsor was, he begged forgiveness for having been a member of the party that arrested Mây's father. Father

Peter assured him there was nothing to forgive. The man had been pressed into military service against his will and could not do otherwise than obey the orders of his officer. The same fate had befallen another of Mây's nephews, who, conscripted into the Vietnamese Army as many others were, had sacrificed his life during the invasion of Cambodia which freed that country from the murderous Khmer Rouge regime.

When the official Canadian refugee acceptance program came to an end, a new charitable association was formed by Father Hồ and the Van Bourgondien couple. The mission of the new organization was to help meet the needs of Catholic churches, schools and religious orders in southern Việt Nam through material aid and moral support. In several communities where the Soeurs de la Providence served, the Sisters each received subsistence support in the amount of three hundred dollars a year, admittedly very little in absolute terms, but a great deal in the way of moral support. Other funds were allocated to furthering Christian education, with special help for those pupils who might eventually enter into the service of the Church.

Thus it was that Father Hồ spent his years at Saint Andrew's in the triple service of the Parish in general, the ever-growing Vietnamese community in Victoria and the Church in Việt Nam. In 1994, Father Peter elected to move to Saint Patrick's Parish, the second largest in the Victoria Diocese, where he would assist Monsignor Philip Hanley, who, because his health had declined somewhat, was no longer able to assume all of his former duties.

Founded in 1912 as Our Lady of Lourdes Parish, Saint Patrick's acquired a new church and a new name with the construction of a handsome building in 1960. Over the years the Parish had known many devoted and energetic priests whose activities had not been confined within the walls of the church, but rather extended widely into the community. In this they were supported by various voluntary organizations, including the Catholic Women's League, the Knights of Columbus and the Society of Saint Vincent de Paul. As the area around the church evolved from farmland to a suburban residential district, the congregation increased accordingly. Many constructions and improvements were undertaken, including the building of a four-room school in 1956 which soon became a much larger institution after many additions were made to accommodate the ever-increasing enrolment. The Parish also had a tradition of openness and concern for other countries and cultures, having given much support to missionary work, notably in the African country of Sierra Leone. An active chapter of the Canadian Catholic Organization for Development and Peace oversaw various projects to increase awareness of international needs.

Needless to say, Father Hồ found much to do in this stimulating new environment. He enjoyed his association with his wise, understanding and supportive pastor, Monsignor Philip Hanley. He enjoyed his contacts with individual parishioners on the occasion of the momentous events in their lives: weddings, baptisms, confirmations. He shared their pain and offered hope and consolation when they were afflicted or when they grieved over the loss of loved ones. His greatest satisfaction, however, came from the liturgical services over which he presided and the mysterious and powerful emotion that he always felt as an agent of human connection with the Divine Spirit.

XII. Going Home

Mây had not forgotten his Vietnamese parishioners, and he soon organized Masses in Vietnamese on a regular basis at Saint Patrick's, followed by a loyal congregation. Mây's thoughts turned increasingly to his homeland and the family he had left behind so long ago. How he would love to see them again, to embrace his father, now an elderly man, but still the bulwark of his family and the community! How he would love to talk with Tòa and Đỏ and even see his old comrade Father Đệ, who had recently been released from prison! How he would love to be with the whole community as they gathered for Mass in the new village church! It had been nearly fifteen years since that fateful night when the little boat of Tướng and Sồi had slipped through the shadows past the border post, carrying Mây away from all he had known and loved. Reports coming out of Việt Nam seemed to indicate that the persecution of the Church had softened. The current, more moderate leaders of the country had in general replaced the hardliners of the past. Perhaps they had come to realize that there was nothing to be gained by pursuing their vendetta against all forms of religion and the people who represented them. Perhaps they might tolerate the visit of a Canadian Catholic priest in search of his roots and who just happened to have been the object of someone else's persecution fifteen years before. Perhaps... The more Mây thought about it, the more the conviction grew within him that it would be worth the risk to try. He prayed to God over the matter; if it were truly His will that he make this attempt, he would be protected. If not, he would submit to the consequences, as Father Đệ had so bravely done in the course of his life of service to the Church.

Mây contacted his friend and associate, Karel Van Bourgondien, to inquire if he would possibly accept to accompany him on a short trip to Việt Nam, to act as his personal guarantor and to assess those needs of the local population which Ho Missions might address. To his grateful relief, Mây learned that his friend would indeed be pleased to accompany him on his journey, and plans were immediately drawn up to undertake the trip at their earliest mutual convenience.

The Diocese was successful in obtaining a Vietnamese visa for Father Peter Hồ, which was an encouraging sign, and Mây began to consider his upcoming journey with increased optimism, especially since the scope of the trip had become considerably larger: in fact, if all went well in Việt Nam, Father Peter would do no less than circle the globe! He hoped to stop in Bangkok, and then repeat his 1981 flight back to Canada via France, where he would once again visit the shrine at Lourdes. The day of departure arrived. Bolstered by the good wishes and prayers of his parishioners, Mây joined his friend Karel on the first leg of their journey: the short trip over to Vancouver, where they would board a Singapore Airlines flight to that city and thence to Sài Gòn.

The absolute immensity of the Pacific Ocean impressed upon the two travelers the wide gulf between the histories, traditions, languages and cultures of the lands bathed by its waters. Once again Mây thought how small we all are really, each one in his own little corner of the universe, taken up with his or her own day to day problems, yet sharing the universal human condition and the privileged oneness with the Deity which faith inspires.

After changing planes in Singapore, Mây and Karel found themselves heading north over a sparkling South China Sea. Through his window, Mây could perceive the outer reaches of the Cà Mau Peninsula faintly delineated on the horizon. Was that Rạch Giá or Rảy Mới over there on the horizon to the left? Mây's thoughts went back to that time in his youth when he had lived there with his Hainanese parishioners. For a moment, he amused himself trying to think just how you said certain things in the language he had learned with them and which he had now, after these many years, almost forgotten. He realized how much the words of the language we speak are part and parcel of our perception of both physical and spiritual realities, furthermore how much value the Word has in itself: "In the beginning was the Word..." and, in whatever human language the Word may be, "...the Word was with God, and the Word was God. " (St. John 1:1)

As for Father Peter's companion Karel, he was counting on Mây to be his interpreter throughout his visit to the country they were just now beginning to see clearly beneath the wings of their plane: a patchwork of verdant fields criss-crossed by innumerable canals and waterways gleaming brightly in the sunlight. Here and there, the travelers could make out the towns and cities they were passing over. All the names were familiar to Mây: Sóc Trăng, Vĩnh Long, Mỹ Tho... Somewhere over there to the left was Mây's own island with its little village of Tân Hòa. And then, as the plane slowly descended, the dull haze of a great city loomed before them, even as a voice in English and Vietnamese instructed the passengers to fasten their seatbelts and prepare for landing in Sài Gòn, the Pearl of the Orient.

In reality, the voice identified the city by another name...

The airport terminal was busily occupied by passengers coming and going and waiting in lines. The wall behind the immigration counter was draped with a large red banner bearing a yellow star in place of the red-striped yellow flag of former times.

The officer in charge examined Karel Van Bourgondien's Passport and handed it back without a word. Father Peter Hồ's documentation seemed to give him more concern. Taking the passport with him he withdrew from the counter momentarily and spoke briefly into a telephone. When he returned, he begged the good priest to kindly wait a moment. Someone would come to complete the formalities for his entrance into the country. The person appeared moments later and escorted Mây into a paneled room nearby, leaving Karel to wait outside. The interrogation seemed to be taking an inordinate amount of time, and, after half an hour, Karel approached the door to see what was going on. The investigator seemed to be speaking very earnestly to Mây. Finally he returned the passport, and the two men rose and came out the door to the area where Karel was waiting. The investigator then returned to his previous duties, indicating that Mây was free to leave with his companion.

"Well, how did it go?" asked Karel.

"As well as could be expected," replied Mây. "But he asked a lot of questions and finally warned me to be very careful not to take an active part in any public assemblies…including those in churches," he added sadly.

"Come on, Peter," replied Karel. "You're going home. Your family's waiting for you outside the gate."

And truly, there they were: brothers, sisters, nieces, nephews. They had all made the trip by minibus to greet their long lost, dearest Mây and his distinguished companion.

Such an explosion of joy all around! Yet behind it all on such occasions, comes the sobering realization that our life on earth is circumscribed in time: kids grow up, smooth-skinned youths become middle-aged adults, weathered by cares and toil, elders become…they become…

"*Ông bố đâu?* Where's Dad?" asked Mây suddenly.

"Waitng for you at home," came the reply. "He wanted to welcome you in our own house, not on some parking lot!"

With Mây making the presentations, Karel Van Bourgondien was introduced to each member of the Hồ family, and their warm welcome could be felt shining through the air of formality required by such circumstances. Then everyone piled into the minibus, and the hired driver vehicled them through the city's incredible traffic to the home of Mr. Vũ Chới, a friend of the family, where they would all spend the night before setting out for home the following morning.

On the way home the next day, their minibus dropped them off in Mỹ Tho City for a brief call on Bishop Phạm Minh Mẫn, presently a Cardinal, whom Mây was later to welcome in Victoria on the occasion of the Cardinal's visit to Canada. Then it was back on the road again for Đồng Tháp Province. At An Long town, they thanked their minibus driver and took the ferry across the river to their island, where the whole party mounted on a strange assortment of motorcycles and, in a cloud of smoke, fumes and dust, sped off in the direction of Tân Hòa village.

The lengthening shadows of dusk had plunged the house in relative obscurity, and Mây stood a moment in the doorway, his eyes adjusting to the dimness of the light. Someone was stirring in a darkened corner, and then a familiar voice called out:

"Con trai Mây đấy không? Is that you, Mây?"

The upright figure of Mây's father, shirtless in the closeness of the warm evening air, emerged into the fading light, his eighty years diminishing neither the sureness of his step nor the firmness of his embrace. Mây briefly contemplated the lined face, the broad smile, the clear, steadfast gaze, and drew his father once again into his arms.

"Ông bố..."

And then, as all the family gathered round, lamps were lit, Karel was given a place in the family circle, and everyone looked to Mây expectantly. Mây told them how tremendously happy he was to be back home again, how proud and honored he was to have such a warm, loving family, how fortunate he had been to have such strong, godly parents. He expressed his heartfelt gratitude to his father and evoked the memory of his loving mother, whom many of the younger ones had never known. Then, as *Linh mục,* Father Phê-rô Hồ led them all in a solemn prayer of thanksgiving and supplication.

The days that followed were filled with visits to and from local parishioners and people Mây had known fifteen years before. One can imagine with how much joy Mây was reunited with Father Đệ, as they talked at length about the times they had spent together and their vastly different lives since the frightful day of Đệ's arrest.

In the village, Mây inquired as to the whereabouts of Tướng and Sồi, the two lads who had engineered his successful escape and transportation to Phnom Penh. "Oh, they're somewhere off in Cambodia," was the reply, and Mây was given to understand that it was best he not know the exact nature of their present occupations. Mây imagined them sealing some suspicious business deal with two pineapples and a bottle of rum, and decided not to pursue his inquiry any further. Nevertheless, in his mind, he sent them a silent message of thanks for all their efforts on his behalf.

Along with Karel, Mây paid a visit to the local school and met the head teacher and his staff, who took them on a tour of the building. There were six spacious class-rooms, each accommodating thirty or more pupils, who, while all neatly brushed and attired in their school clothes, were either balancing on rickety stools or spread out on the floor amid a scattering of books and papers. "Very nice," commented Mây, "But we've got to do something to get these kids some proper furniture," he added as Karel nodded in agreement. These words were immediately translated into actions, and Mây and Karel set about buying wood and rounding up a crew of local carpenters. Within a month, at a cost of about $1500, all the classrooms were equipped with beautifully built desks and benches. It was money well spent, for not only did the school have proper furniture, but a number of families had benefited from the employment its construction had afforded. Each of the teachers and workmen came around to thank Mây and Karel for their generous contribution.

There were other needs in the community, many just as pressing, and Mây and Karel did their best to help. Eight tons of rice were ordered to help feed the poorest families as well as 105 kilograms of pork for undernourished children. More than two thousand dollars were spent to help repair the road leading to the church. Funds were however not inexhaustible, and many things would just have to wait for a future visit. Mây promised himself he would be back as soon as Ho Missions could round up some additional contributions.

It was a great satisfaction to Mây to see that, in spite of past persecutions of the Church, the people's faith remained strong. Masses were well attended, and the Church played an active role in the community. Yet the horizon was not entirely clear. Although Mây had been briefly permitted to celebrate Mass in his own home, this permission was soon rescinded by the village authorities when the number of people attending began to get out of hand. It was of course out of the question for Mây to celebrate Mass in the church in light of the admonitions he had received on entering the country. Some time in the future, perhaps... but not just yet.

The time came for Mây and Karel to end their visit. The inevitable sadness of their departure was, however, tempered by Mây's resolve to return in the near future.

Karel would now fly back directly from Sài Gòn to Vancouver; Mây would continue on to Bangkok, where he hoped to see his old friend from Saint Paul University, Father Peter Surin.

Unfortunately, during his fifteen years abroad, Mây had apparently lost some of his natural immunities to the various bugs that inhabit the waters of one's homeland, wherever that may be, and which seem to attack visitors and tourists with great glee. On his arrival in Bangkok, Mây fell so ill that he remained confined to his hotel room for a good part of his stay. A weak voice on the telephone informed Father Peter Surin of the alarming condition of his homonym, and the good Father rushed to Mây's bedside, half expecting to be called upon to perform last rites. He was relieved to find Mây's affliction entirely curable and proceeded to organize a visit to a nearby hospital where the patient was given appropriate medication. In a few days, Father Peter Hồ was back on his feet, and he and Father Peter Surin enjoyed reminiscing about their days together at the University and discussing their current challenges and endeavours. Soon it was time for Mây to take his plane again. Father Surin drove him to the airport where friendly goodbyes were exchanged. Now entirely relieved of his momentary indisposition, Mây thanked Father Surin for all the help he had given in getting his old companion back in traveling shape and for his enduring friendship over the years.

The long flight to Paris brought back many memories of Mây's first air voyage from Bangkok to the City of Light. How long ago that now seemed! So much had happened in the intervening years, so many places, so many people. Father Hồ's thoughts turned again to his parishioners at Saint Patrick's, whom he would soon be seeing again. It was with his home parish in mind that he took the train from Paris to the town of Lourdes and its famous shrine.

It will be remembered that the first name given to Saint Patrick's was Our Lady of Lourdes. As recounted in the Parish annals[12], it was here at Lourdes, one day in the early years of the 20th century that a certain Father J.A. Vullinghs had stood in adoration at the grotto of Our Lady. Father Vullinghs was a native of Holland and a graduate of Louvain University, who had been serving the parishes of Vancouver Island for the previous twenty years and who was visiting relatives in Europe. While praying at the grotto, Father Vullinghs was struck with the desire to create a similar place of adoration of the Blessed Virgin on his far off Canadian island. No sooner had he taken this resolve, so the story goes, than he was approached by a mysterious Spanish noblewoman who, on becoming acquainted with Father Vullingh's desire, offered to donate a statue of the Virgin from among her art treasures, for the adornment of the proposed grotto. Whatever the exact origin of the statue or the conditions of its miraculous transportation to Vancouver Island may be, the fact remains that when Our Lady of Lourdes Parish was established some years later with Father Vullinghs as its first Pastor, his grotto was eventually constructed with the statue in the place of honour. When

---

[12] Mona Macgillivray and Edith Spohn, *The History of Our Lady of Lourdes – St. Patrick's, from 1911 - 1992*, Victoria, 1992.

the new Saint Patrick's Church was built in 1960, the statue was moved to a position within the church, to the left of the main altar, where it stands today. It became both an object of veneration and a symbol of the affiliation of the parishioners with their church. The statue is indeed a truly beautiful one, and Father Peter had admired it on a daily basis. It was only appropriate therefore that his visit to Lourdes be both a homage to the man who had founded the new parish and a sign of Father Peter's own commitment to serve its present congregation. It was also an occasion to remember the good works of Father Guy Merveille, who had so generously brought Mây to the sources of his faith, to this and other sacred places, at the time of Mây's difficult adaptation to life outside the confines of his previously known world. Refreshed and with renewed conviction, Father Peter returned to his duties at Saint Patrick's in Victoria. However, he could not soon forget his concerns for the people in Việt Nam and he was already planning in his mind the next trip back to his homeland.

A little more than a year later, Mây was back in that paneled interrogation room beside the customs and immigration counter at Sài Gòn Airport. An extra bag he had been carrying, containing some medical supplies and other items donated by the parishioners of Saint Patrick's had just been confiscated by Customs as illegal importa-tions, and Mây was now waiting for the interrogator to return after remaining alone in the room for more than an hour. Was it some old animosity that Mây's previous visit had awakened, or was the investigator being unusually zealous, or was it simply that the data base on the Vietnamese computers had been improved over the last year? Something was going on in any case, and Mây's agitation increased as he waited. Finally the official returned with Mây's passport and a computer print-out. He opened the passport and looked suspiciously at the opening page.

Raising his eyebrows, he read the name, *"Pe Ter Ho…"*, forcing the English pronunciation. His expression turned to a frown as he continued in Vietnamese: *"Linh Mục ở Ca Na Đa phải không?"*

Mây nodded affirmatively.

The official glanced at his computer print-out. This supposed Peter Ho, was he not in reality one Hồ Văn Mây, suspected of subversive activities after the Liberation in the Province of Đồng Tháp? Was he not the associate of the known renegade and convicted criminal Nguyễn Văn Đệ? Had he not himself been arrested on one occasion in 1979? And had he not then slipped out of the country illegally to continue his subversive actions abroad?

Visibly shaken, Mây freely admitted to his identity, but insisted that he was in no way engaged in any subversive activity. He had simply come to visit his family and to support the humanitarian efforts of the Catholic Church in Việt Nam.

The official gathered up his papers and left the room again, leaving Mây to wait a further two hours before his return.

When he came back, the investigator continued the same line of interrogation as before, but was unable to obtain any confession from Mây as to his supposed criminal activities. These periodic visits continued on into the evening until, finally, the investigator, seeing his working day coming to an end, appeared to have reached a decision. He handed back Mây's passport and delivered his verdict. Seeing that Hồ Văn Mây was now a Canadian citizen and that the accusations against him were for the moment unconfirmed, he would be allowed to continue his visit, which was to be as brief as possible. Any further visits to the country in the near future would be viewed with great suspicion by the authorities, and he recommended that *Linh Mục Pe Ter Ho* confine his priestly activities to Canada for the time being.

Outside the gate, Mây finally joined members of his family who had been waiting more than seven hours.

It would be another ten years before Father Peter dared to again present himself at that Customs and Immigration counter.

XIII. The Guide

The succeeding years at Saint Patrick's brought to Father Peter Hồ both the joy of a committed life of service and the usual lot of difficulties and disappointments from which no human existence is exempt.

As the new century dawned, Saint Patrick's Parish was going through a rather trying period in its long and eventful evolution. Commitments toward a major building program, compounded by financial difficulties on the Diocesan level, demanded a great deal of attention on the part of the Parish Council. A much appreciated and long-standing priest and pastor, Father Hill, was involved in a serious motor accident and temporarily incapacitated. Monsignor Philip Hanley, the greatly loved and respected parish priest, carried on manfully in his role, but age and failing health meant that the day was coming when he would be physically unable to continue. When that day eventually arrived, the Bishop and the Clergy Personnel Committee turned their attention to the problem of a replacement. An appointment was duly made and the new priest arrived to assume his duties. Unfortunately, space constraints within the rectory required that Father Hồ vacate his quarters and take up residence in a private dwelling, a necessity he accepted with no small measure of personal sorrow, but to which he was resigned, in the interests, however obscure, of the Parish in general.

The new pastorship was not, however, a lengthy one, and was followed by another of equal brevity. In all sincerity, the men concerned had long pondered the extent of their commitment to the Church and eventually reconsidered their calling completely.

Now Bishop Raymond Roussin turned to Father Hồ. Would Peter kindly come down to the Pastoral Center, as there was an important matter they should discuss. Somewhat surprised by this sudden interest on the part of the Chancery, given the absence of any significant contacts over the past months, Father Peter went down to meet the Bishop as requested.

"Peter," began the Bishop on a fatherly tone, "I know how much of an inconvenience this has been for you, having to live away on your own and all. I think it's time you moved back into the rectory. It is after all your rightful place."

Father Peter had no objection, but he did remind the Bishop that the needs of the Parish pastor and his associates had necessitated his departure in the first place and that there was simply no more room in the rectory.

"Well that was true enough," replied the Bishop, "but the current pastor will be leaving shortly, and I am asking you to take his place, for a year as administrator, and after that as the standing pastor of Saint Patrick's Parish."

Completely dumbfounded, Father Peter could only stammer out a request to be given time to think it over. The Bishop, however, had already risen and was going out the door. "Time, you want? Yes certainly, it's an important decision. I'll give you plenty of time. How about until tomorrow morning? Sleep on it." And he was gone.

Mây was so preoccupied by the Bishop's proposition that he almost went through a red light as he was maneuvering his tired old Volvo back towards Saint Patrick's Church. Maybe this was a sign that there are times when one should stop and not rush blindly ahead toward some illusory destination. How could he possibly imagine himself in charge of Saint Patrick's Parish? Oh, he could handle the mechanics of the job all right, but what would the parishioners think? It was a symbolic thing. Father Peter was after all, as the immigration officer had pointed out, only Hồ Văn Mây, a person born and raised in another country, from another culture, with another language. Shouldn't the parish pastor come out of the flock he intends to serve? By the time Mây pulled up in front of the church, he had almoșt made up his mind to decline the Bishop's offer. He was overcome with fatigue, but rather than sleep on it, as the Bishop had put it, it would be best to pray on it, and Mây went into the darkened sanctuary to do just that.

As he was sitting quietly in one of the front pews, he felt a hand on his shoulder. It was Monsignor Hanley who had come to join him in this place they both knew so well.

"I understand congratulations are in order, Peter," he began. "The Bishop called to tell me you'll be the next pastor here."

"No, I don't think so, Monsignor. You see, I've thought a lot about it, and I don't think I'm qualified. I come from another country with different customs and traditions. I still have a language problem. I don't have enough experience. I'm not…"

Monsignor Hanley cut him off: "Nonsense, Peter. Coming from a normally intelligent man, I have never heard such pure unadulterated pap! I thought you knew what Catholic meant. Universal, have you forgotten? It doesn't matter what country you come from or what your accent is. We are all one before God. The Bishop needs you, the Church needs you and this parish needs you. You must accept."

Mây looked up. "Do you really think so?"

"Yes, I really think so," was the reply. "I know so."

The next morning Mây called on the Bishop to accept the new appointment.

Father Peter realized, as if he did not know before, that the life of a parish depends on the contributions of many persons: deacons and associates, altar servers, ushers, parish councilors, catechism teachers, musicians, choir leaders and singers, members of the various service and charitable organizations. Some commitments are momentary, others span over decades. Father Peter's own life was fuller than ever before. In addition to the Sunday Masses, including the special service for his Vietnamese parishioners, Father Peter held daily noon Masses throughout the week. Many of the same people attended every day, so that Father Peter got to know them and miss them if they were not there. Others were tourists, vacationers or visitors, seen once or twice before they went on to other destinations. Some were filled with sorrow and remorse, in need of the reassurance of the Church's eternal promise; some came to strengthen their resolve to change and better their existences, some came out of joy and thankfulness for the fullness of their lives. With all of them, Father Peter felt a special bond during Mass. What could the good Father do without Mass? It was his life. It was being a priest.

There were, however, occasions when Father Peter was overcome by a great sense of personal loss. One of these had come even before he had assumed his duties as parish priest when, on February 24th 2001, he received the news that his father had passed away on the way home from Sài Gòn, after being hospitalized there. The last words of the dying man had been two almost identical syllables: *Mẹ* and *Mây*: *Đức Mẹ* and *Con trai Mây*, Holy Mary and my son Mây... In the hour of his death, Hồ Văn Ngự prayed that these two might intervene for him as he presented himself before the Lord. On hearing this, Mây was so distraught, he broke down in tears during the Mass. On his last visit to Việt Nam he had helped to construct a little house for his father where he could be more at ease in his old age; now his father had a new dwelling in the house of the Lord. Yet Mây would miss him greatly.

The second moment of profound loss came on June 20th, 2004. Only months before, Mây had sponsored a visit to Victoria for his two brothers, Đỏ and Toà. His younger brother Đỏ, already suffering from an incurable cancer, had refused any treatment in Canada, and died shortly after his return to Việt Nam, leaving a wife and six children. Mây had always been particularly close to Đỏ; his sorrow was all the greater in that it revived the memory of Mây's beloved mother Phạn and how Đỏ had so gallantly come to her defense outside the Seminary in Cái Răng Remembering what he had said to Đỏ, "I'll love you forever", Mây promised to take care of his children, that they might live their lives in the image of their father, with all his lifelong qualities of loyalty and generosity.

On these occasions and on others, Mây reflected on the course of his own life over the years. It had been quite a journey. A benevolent Guide, far greater than any of the human ones Mây had known, had taken him up by the hand on the delta of the Mekong and led him away over many roads and through many lands. The only fee to be paid was faith in the Guide and the ultimate destination. Sometimes the lands they crossed were lushly verdant and bountiful; at other times they went over terrible, devastated plains and through desolate, ruined cities. Yes, there had been occasions when Mây had shouted to the Guide to stop and let him sit by the side of the road for a moment. But these stopovers were

soon interrupted by a call from the Guide: "Let's get
going again!" and the journey resumed. Many travelers
had joined them as they went along. Some came with a
cold heart, and when they trudged together in unfeeling
silence and animosity, the Guide too was silent and
pushed on relentlessly. But when kindness and charity
reigned among them, the Guide seemed to love them all
the more and sent them signs of hope and encouragement.
Although the Guide seemed to have a plan for each
traveler, his path was not traced out on some enduring
map of destiny. When they came to a fork in the road, the
Guide would ask, "Where shall we go from here? What
road shall we take? Who shall we meet along the way?"

Yes, Mây realized, God the Guide had sustained him
throughout his life journey. He had done this in many
ways, acting through many human intermediaries. Now,
as a priest, Mây had become one of those privileged
intermediaries and this power and this responsibility
never ceased to fill him with awe and wonder. Had not it
all been clearly put forth by Jesus himself in the Gospel
of Saint Matthew?

*And Jesus went about all the cities and villages,
teaching in their Synagogues, and preaching the
gospel of the kingdom, and healing every sickness and
every disease among the people. But when he saw the
multitudes, he was moved with compassion on them,
because they fainted and were scattered abroad, as
sheep having no shepherd. Then saith he unto his*

disciples, the harvest truly is plenteous, but the laborers are few; pray ye therefore the Lord of the harvest, that he will send forth laborers into the harvest. (St. Matthew 9:35-38)

But Mây was persuaded that this power and responsibility was not confined to priests and other religious figures, but could rather be shared with anyone else on the planet. "I believe," Father Hồ confided to a friend, "that God has a general will for all of us, which is this: 'make your life an act of love!' He wants us to make the power of love dictate all our decisions and guide us in all our actions. That does not mean that He makes all of our choices for us. To a certain extent, we have to think for ourselves and bear our own responsibilities. Sometimes the decisions we have to make are very difficult ones; sometimes we hesitate to seize the opportunities God opens up for us. Here we should try to consult with God so that we may see how his general will applies to the specific decision we have to make."

Thinking of his own personal experience, Father Peter continued: "I am convinced that it is possible to do God's will only on one condition. I have to believe that God knows more than I do about what will make me truly happy. If God had given me everything I ever asked for, I have the feeling that I would now be seriously unhappy. Ultimately, our lives are in God's hands. And when those moments arrive when we are called on to bestow our special act of love, God will speak to our hearts,"

Here he paused and added, "…the important thing is to cultivate a listening heart."

These were convictions Mây held from his own loving parents, his people and the servants of the Church in his own country, and which, reinforced by all of Mây's experience abroad, he continued to live by.

The Guide was waiting for Mây to join him for yet another leg of the journey. Ten years after Mây's last, frightening visit to Việt Nam, all signs coming out of the country seemed to point toward a growing tolerance of religious expression on the part of the authorities. That's what Mây had thought the last time, but possibly now it was different. Should he risk another visit to his homeland? Yes, he decided and resolved to apply to the Bishop for permission to undertake another trip to Việt Nam. Permission was granted and the ever-obliging travel agency booked a ticket for Father Hồ to Hong Kong and Sài Gòn via Cathay Pacific Airlines on May 10th 2006.

It was decided within the Parish to honour Father Peter and wish him well on his journey on the occasion of the annual Saint Patrick's Day dinner. Before a large gathering of parishioners and well-wishers, Mr. Vince Cain undertook to deliver the traditional "roast" of the guest of honour. This is a North American tradition consisting of a light-hearted account of some of the victim's foibles and qualities and intended as a mark of deep down affection and admiration. After recounting a few amusing anecdotes drawn from their long standing friendship, Mr. Cain concluded by remarking that one always knew when Father Peter's homilies were coming to an end when he said, "My dear brothers and sisters..." True enough, such is the structure of the sermon. But after this announcement comes the essential message, spoken in tones of great sincerity and conviction; then, in Father Peter's resonant voice, the first words of the Apostles' Creed: "I believe in God!"

"My dear brothers and sisters..." and... "I believe in God."

Fraternity and Faith.

Are not these two of the cornerstones of a Christian life?

Speaking on behalf of all the parishioners, Mr. Paul Redchurch wished Father Hồ well on his forthcoming trip and assured him that everyone's prayers would accompany him on each day of his journey and mission.

We do not know what difficulties if any Father Peter Hồ Văn Mây encountered at the airport in Sài Gòn, but we do know through word received by his nephew Tuyển, that Father Peter arrived in Tân Hòa village on a Saturday evening, and that he celebrated the Sunday Mass the next morning in his own parish church, before the entire congregation which had assembled to welcome him home.

Would it be permitted to imagine that, from somewhere in the universal heavens, a mother and a father were looking down and shedding their love upon that assembly?

Mây's mother, Lê Thị Phạn   Mây's father, Hồ Văn Ngự

Mây at Saint Sulpice Seminary, age 23

Festive supper at Mây's home on the occasion of his ordination as a priest, 1985.

Congratulations to the newly ordained priest

Tân Hòa Village, Đồng Tháp Province

Entrance portal to Mây's home

Mây, refugee at the Phanat Nikhom Holding Center in Thailand, 1981

Mây, student at Saint Paul University, Ottawa, 1984

Father Peter, Karel Van Bourgondien
and the Sisters of Divine Providence, 1995

Father Peter and Father Đê, 1995

Father Peter and the children of Bến Dinh Parish, 1995

Father Peter Hồ, pastor of Saint Patrick's Church, Victoria, Canada

ISBN 142510790-7